HOW DO TEACHERS COMMUNICATE?
A Review and Critique of Assessment Practices

Joseph L. McCaleb
Editor

Published by

**CLEARINGHOUSE
ON TEACHER
EDUCATION**

American Association of Colleges for Teacher Education
One Dupont Circle, Suite 610, Washington, DC
20036

May 1987

CITE AS:
McCaleb, Joseph L. (Ed.) (1987). *How Do Teachers Communicate? A Review and Critique of Assessment Practices* (Teacher Education Monograph No. 7). Washington, DC: ERIC Clearinghouse on Teacher Education.

MANUSCRIPTS:
The ERIC Clearinghouse on Teacher Education invites individuals to submit proposals for writing monographs for the Teacher Education Monograph Series. Proposals should include:

1. A detailed manuscript proposal of not more than five pages.
2. A vita.
3. A writing sample.

ORDERS:
The price for a single copy, including fourth class postage and handling, is $9.50. For first class postage, add $1.00 for each copy ordered. Orders must be prepaid.

Order from:
ERIC CLEARINGHOUSE ON TEACHER EDUCATION
American Association of Colleges for Teacher Education
One Dupont Circle, NW, Suite 610
Washington, DC 20036
(202) 293-2450

Library of Congress Catalog Card Number: 87-81069

ISBN 0-89333-046-9

Series Editor: Elizabeth A. Ashburn, Ph.D.

Office of Educational
Research and Improvement
U.S. Department of Education

This publication was prepared with funding from the Office of Educational Research and Improvement, U.S. Department of Education under Contract No. 400-86-0033. The opinions expressed in this report do not necessarily reflect the positions or policies of OERI or DOE.

Contents

Acknowledgments

Many persons contributed to the development of this monograph. Members of the Committee on Assessment and Testing in the Speech Communication Association have patiently supported and critiqued my studies of teachers' communications for several years. I especially recognize Don Boileau, education director of SCA, for offering financial assistance and personally arranging to move reluctant notions toward publication. Richard Arends, chair of the Department of Curriculum & Instruction, and Patti Gillespie, chair of the Department of Communication Arts & Theatre, at the University of Maryland provided financial support and personal encouragement.

My contacts in state departments of education have been invaluable, readily sharing their instruments and correcting my interpretations. A short list of those who were especially generous in offering their expertise and time in responding to drafts includes: Gail Tomala in Connecticut, Betty Fry in Florida, Lester Solomon in Georgia, Louise Tanney and Pat Ortman in Maryland, Kathy Thomas in South Carolina, George Malo in Tennessee, Susan Barnes in Texas, and Nancy Vance in Virginia.

I have special appreciation for the chapter authors who were punctual and friendly in meeting deadlines and developed ideas beyond my expectations. Finally, I am happy to acknowledge the superb editorial assistance provided by the ERIC Clearinghouse on Teacher Education: Betsy Ashburn, former Clearinghouse director and now with the Office of Educational Research and Improvement, personalized the publishing process and gave incisive, substantive suggestions; and Joan Barrett, Clearinghouse editor, continued to unify the work substantively and stylistically.

Joseph L. McCaleb
University of Maryland

Introduction

Communication paradoxically belongs to everyone and to no one. Because we spend so much time talking and listening, communication becomes commonplace. Everyone assumes expertise and confidently diagnoses communication problems and prescribes remedies. Unfortunately, because communication—the process of creating shared meanings among individuals who have diverse characteristics and experiences—is complex and intricate, these simple prescriptions often fail. Communication thus belongs to no one. Teachers and students often talk but do not understand each other.

The purpose of this monograph is to improve communication. By first acknowledging that we do not comprehend the complexity of teachers' communication, we can begin by trying to develop a conceptual understanding of this extremely important interpersonal, dynamic event. One way to manage this difficult task is to focus on communication in instructional settings. Although instructional communication shares features with communication in other settings such as the home, office, or shopping center, its unique characteristics are best captured by looking closely at the classroom. We do this by using communication and instructional theory to examine assessment strategies that have recently been designed. Finally, implications are drawn for the improvement of communication.

We focus specifically upon the assessment of communication for four primary reasons:

1. Communication is essential to teaching.
2. Almost every state now requires formal assessment of teachers for initial or for continuing certification, and almost all assessments claim to evaluate communication abilities.
3. The term "communication" is used in many ways, and the extent to which primary dimensions of communication are incorporated into the assessments is not evident.
4. A description and critique of the ways communication has been conceptualized and assessed can inform preservice and inservice programs as well as evaluation designs.

Each of these reasons deserves elaboration. First, the importance of communication is generally acknowledged. For example, B. O. Smith includes communication as one of the six competencies needed by all teachers in *A Design for a School of Pedagogy*. Denemark and Nutter stated in *A Case for Extended Programs of Initial Teacher Preparation*, "Communication skills are central to relating not only to students but also to professional colleagues, parents, and other community representatives . . . It requires listening and reading skills as well as speaking and writing facility" (pp. 19–20). Finally, AACTE's *Educating a Profession: Profile of a Beginning Teacher* (February 1983) asserts, "A teacher's ability to communicate effectively is essential" (p. 5). The emphasis in our analysis is upon oral communication (speaking and listening), but similarities are often found to other forms of communication (particularly, reading and writing).

The second and third reasons concern how the assessment of teachers' communications has become so extensive and simultaneously how the assessments have emerged with rather diverse characteristics. Within the past decade, more than half the 50 states have implemented assessments that include some measure of communication ability. The meaning of "communication," however, differs considerably among the states. At one extreme, the process of teaching and the process of communication appear almost synonymous. States that have adopted a narrative approach to performance assessment (the observer writes an account of what is happening in the classroom) accept this global view of communication. At the other extreme, observers use an instrument that requires counting the frequency of particular communication behaviors such as blatant mispronunciations. If judged by one instrument, the teacher might be labeled an effective communicator, but the same teacher could be called ineffective when the other instrument is used. Plans for improving communication will obviously differ considerably depending on the conception of communication. By describing and critiquing the assessments, these conceptions can be identified and improvement strategies can be better designed.

The fourth reason for developing this monograph suggests that certain audiences should find the contents useful. The territory overlapped by communication and instruction has not been carefully delineated. The development of our understanding of teachers' praise illustrates the unfolding of complexities within an important concept that is under the domains of both instruction and communication. Not long ago, teachers were urged to always find the positive in students' ideas and seldom, if ever, to be critical (e.g., Diederich, 1963). Through closer study with principles from learning theory and communication theory, we now understand much more about the discriminating use of praise and criticism (e.g., Brophy, 1981). This monograph identifies other critical variables that merit close scrutiny.

Statewide assessments represent an enormous investment of public opinion and professional expertise in the formulation of competency lists, refinement of assessment strategies, and subsequent adjustments made after implementation. About 12 states have engaged in this expensive, time-consuming ordeal in order to develop consensus upon the ingredients of good teaching. By synthesizing their conclusions, significant landmarks in the communication/instruction territory are identified for the consideration of researchers and teachers.

Another audience for this monograph should be those involved in teacher evaluation. According to Phi Delta Kappa's newsletter (Joekel, 1986, p. 1), "Competency assessment of teachers or teachers in training is occurring in 46 states; only one state has no plans to do so." At least 10 states are developing or giving serious consideration to adopting performance assessments. Persons developing these systems can benefit from seeing the numerous ways that communication has been included in existing assessments. The critiques of these approaches may be even more valuable as they elaborate issues that often escape detection. Many states delegate the responsibility for teacher evaluation to the local level. Persons involved at any level in teacher appraisal or supervision can incorporate ideas about teachers' communications from this synthesis and criticism of existing assessments.

As stated earlier, communication appears to be the province of everyone. The unstated assumption is that because we spend so much time talking and listening we have considerable knowledge, even expertise, in communication (Adler, 1983). Why should we devote special inquiry to this common activity? While our lay expertise is often adequate for common everyday use, more specialized expertise is needed to develop an assessment strategy that makes precise distinctions, collectively composes the essential features of effective communication, and incorporates the unique characteristics of the classroom.

The danger of a casual, unstudied approach to communication can be illustrated with a brief historical reference and with a common experience in teacher preparation. Communication has often been split into matters of style and those of substance, and the lay expert appears to be more conscious of style. Plato decried the Sophists who won their lawsuits by giving more attention to style than to the discovery of truth (Clarke, 1953). When preservice teachers are asked to critique a peer's microteaching, they typically emphasize eye contact and vocalized pauses (e.g., "ums" and "uhs")—matters of style. Less obvious but perhaps more critical aspects of communication, such as the quality of the explanation given or the precision of feedback, receive little or no attention from the casual observer.

When policymakers or professional educators design and adopt tests for teachers that include measures of communication ability, they may believe that they have sufficient knowledge of effective speaking and listening to judge the quality of the assessment without seeking additional information or expertise. Because communication appears to be the property of each person, it sometimes has been neglected, left unstudied, or combined with other instruction features. Therefore, we conclude that oral communication deserves separate and specialized study.

Finally, in reviewing the studies of communication and teacher assessment we have been unable to identify any project resembling the scope of this monograph. No one has systematically described the ways that communication has been conceptualized in these assessments. For example, *Teacher Competence* (published in Phi Delta Kappa's Hot Topic Series for 1984–85) included about 50 articles. Although communication is frequently mentioned, none of the articles focus significantly upon its conceptualization or assessment.

Therefore, this monograph is designed to increase our understanding of communication. We do not pretend to be seeking the single best meaning but do expect that a close inspection of the uses of the term can be illuminating. By looking at statewide assessments, we can see more clearly how communication has been conceptualized in *practice*. To establish a basis for comparison, we then describe the ways that communication has been conceptualized in theory and research related to instructional communication. The match and mismatch between practice and theory are then appraised from several vantage points.

The monograph is structured according to the following questions:

1. *What kinds of meaning have been given to communication through the operational definitions found in statewide assessments?*

The first chapter contains a review and analysis of standardized measures and performance assessments of teachers' communications. Twelve communication categories emerge from an inspection of the performance assessments. The numerous meanings given to communication are further elaborated by an examination of differences within each category. Although the categories display considerable variation, the practices of assessment generally portray the teacher as speaker, the sender of messages, rather than as a participant in a transactional process.

2. *What kinds of meaning have been given to communication in the theory and research on communication?*

While the first chapter focuses on practice, chapter 2 shifts to an examination of theory and research. Feezel examines the literature on instructional communication and develops a model with five critical skill areas. He shows how these areas are used for five functions (purposes) and in different modes or patterns of communicating.

3. *What conclusions can be drawn by applying critical perspectives to the ways that teachers' communications have been conceptualized and assessed?*

4

The final three chapters discuss limitations in our current measures of communication. Brown uses the perspective of the communication theorist and linguist to identify important dimensions of communication that have received little, if any, attention in the assessments. For example, is any attention given to the critical ability of the teacher to engage in role taking and then to produce adaptive communication?

According to their developers, most performance assessments are grounded in research on teaching effectiveness. The final two chapters in the monograph explore this claim. Book and Duffy find important relationships between the assessments and the research but also remind us of research limitations related to complexity, context, and curriculum. They also identify limitations of that research paradigm and proceed to explore implications for communication from an information-processing model. Clift also begins with the teaching effectiveness research but helps us reconceptualize communication by modifying the metaphor. The shift enables us to better recognize both the values and limitations of existing conceptualizations.

References

Adler, M. J. (1983). *How to speak; How to listen.* New York: Macmillan.

American Association of Colleges of Teacher Education. (1983). *Educating a professional: Profile of a beginning teacher.* Washington, DC: Author.

Brophy, J. (1981). Teacher praise: A functional analysis. *Review of Educational Research, 51,* 5–32.

Clarke, M. L. (1953). *Rhetoric at Rome.* London: Cohen & West, LTD.

Denemark, G., & Nutter, N. (1980). *The case for extended programs of initial teacher preparation.* Washington, DC: ERIC Clearinghouse for Teacher Education.

Diederich, P. B. (1963). In praise of praise. *NEA Journal, 52,* 58–59.

Joekel, R. (1986). Tracking the reform movement. *News, Notes, and Quotes, 31* (2), 1.

Phi Delta Kappa. (1984–1985). *Teacher Competence.* Bloomington, IN: Author.

Smith, B. O. (1980). *A design for a school of pedagogy.* Washington, DC: U.S. Department of Education.

1

A Review Of Communication Competencies Used In Statewide Assessments

Joseph L. McCaleb

University of Maryland

For at least the past decade, many forces have combined to produce a demand for testing teachers. These forces include a real or perceived decline in student performance, concern for the quality of persons entering the teaching profession, and questions about the quality of the preparation offered in teacher education programs. The demands are evident in recent reform initiatives such as the Holmes' Group report (1986) prepared by deans of colleges of education, the Carnegie Commission report (1986) prepared by numerous political and educational leaders, and "Time for Results," the National Governors' Association report (1986). Each group calls for national standards for teachers.

Statewide assessment of teachers has already been implemented in almost every state. These assessments range from standardized testing to performance evaluation. The pervasiveness of standardized testing is indicated by the widespread adoption of the National Teachers Examinations (NTE). In 1986, 31 states used some form of these examinations, which include tests of basic skills, general knowledge, pedagogical knowledge, communication skills, and subject area specializations (Educational Testing Service [ETS], personal communication, August 7, 1986). Many of the remaining 19 states have designed their own examinations. In addition to the standardized testing, performance assessments have been implemented in 9 states and are currently being considered or developed in 10 others (Joekel, 1986; Ortman & Tanney, 1986).

Statewide assessments offer an extremely valuable resource for studying the characteristics of teachers' communications. The focus on the state level is selected not necessarily because the assessments are better than others but because of the process used to develop and adopt the assessments. Typically, adoption involves a lengthy process of public hearings and professional scrutiny as the proposed competencies are exposed to the diverse constituencies within the state, which include rural and urban interests as well as numerous cultural and ethnic perspectives. This scrutiny is then culminated in the crucible of application—does the assessment survive the tests of feasibility? What emerges from such an ordeal seldom reflects the initial ideals but embodies the results of a democratic process and certainly merits our serious attention.

Assessments conducted at the state level are also important because of their scope. A significant number of teachers and professional educators are involved in statewide activities. For these reasons, an examination of statewide assessments can reveal much about the nature and practical meaning of teachers' communications.

Inquiring about the extent to which these assessments evaluate teachers' communications becomes an elusive search. In basic skills testing, "communication" typically means reading and writing, sometimes includes listening, and almost never has a speaking component. In performance assessment "communication" typically refers to "correct" language usage, pronunciation, and perhaps to certain speech mechanics such as pitch and rate. Important communication variables, however, are often disguised under various competencies with names such as professionalism or instruction. The search for the practical meaning of communication is further complicated by the various procedures used for data collection and interpretation. These complications require a close analysis of specific measures in order to uncover the resources offered through statewide assessment. This analysis is divided into standardized testing and performance assessment.

STANDARDIZED TESTING

Many of the states have adopted basic skills testing, often at the point of entry into a teacher preparation program. Typically, the basic skills test, such as the Pre-Professional Skills Tests developed by the ETS, consists of reading, writing, and mathematics, but omits listening and speaking. A major exception is the Listening Section of the Test of Communication Skills in the NTE's Core Battery. As shown in Table 1, 16 states require the Listening Section.

8

Table 1. Statewide Assessment in Speaking and Listening

State	Listening*	Speaking**	Performance Assessment**	Performance Assessment Planned***
Alabama				X
Arizona				X
Arkansas	X			
Colorado		X		
Connecticut				X
Florida			X	
Georgia			X	
Hawaii	X			
Indiana	X			
Kansas				X
Kentucky	X		X	
Louisiana	X			
Maine	X			
Maryland	X			X
Mississippi	X			X
Missouri				X
Montana	X			
Nebraska				X
New Mexico	X			
New York	X			
N. Carolina	X		X	
Oklahoma			X	
S. Carolina			X	
S. Dakota	X			X
Tennessee	X		X	
Texas			X	
Virginia	X		X	
West Virginia	X	X		
Wisconsin				X

*Information about states using the Listening Section of the NTE Core Battery Examination was provided by the Educational Testing Service.

**Information about states using a test for speaking and performance tests was collected through telephone conversations with representatives from the state departments of education and from the NASDTEC manual (Roth & Mastain, 1984).

***Information about states with plans for performance assessment was provided by Ms. Pat Ortman, who conducted a telephone survey of all 50 states (Ortman & Tanney, 1986).

Statewide standardized testing of speaking occurs in two states. West Virginia uses the College Outcome Measure Project of the American College Testing Program (COMP/ACT). (Details on this test are given later in this section.) Colorado requires prospective teachers to earn a B or better in a performance speech course or to make a speech before three judges. The five-minute presentation is evaluated on language (e.g., standard English usage), delivery, and organization. An increased interest in standardized assessment of oral communication is indicated by the ETS's long-range goal of developing a speaking test.

Because the Listening Section of the NTE's Core Battery is required in 16 states, a description of the test is provided. The test consists of 40 items and requires about 30 minutes to respond to the audiotaped questions. Instructions in the practice booklet (ETS, 1984) state:

> The questions are designed to assess your ability to comprehend oral messages quickly and accurately, to recall and interpret information, and to analyze and evaluate messages.

More specifically, the listening section measures:

- basic comprehension of a message, including paraphrasing of a message, understanding connotations or words, and summarizing major ideas
- analysis of a message, including identifying assumptions, drawing inferences, recognizing implications, and identifying a speaker's tone
- evaluation of a message, including identifying and evaluating logical structure, assessing appropriateness and effectiveness of supporting material, and evaluating the effect of a speaker's tone on an audience
- feedback-response, including identifying appropriate responses to questions or dialogues.

Our analysis of the test placed 50% of the items in basic comprehension, 15% in feedback-response, and the remaining 35% in analysis/evaluation. Stimulus material ranged from listening to conversations that lasted a few seconds to listening to descriptive information that continued as long as 75 seconds. The audiotape has about four different voices, including male, female, and a minority dialect.

The communication assessment portion of COMP/ACT, used by West Virginia, is described by Trank and Steele (1983):

> The COMP assessments of speaking and writing are defined as the ability to communicate about social institutions, science and technology, and the arts. Written and audiotaped stimuli are used as a context for role-playing tasks in which participants write letters to friends, legislators and administrators or speak to friends, informal and formal meetings. Thus three writing samples and three speaking samples are obtained in a variety of realistic contexts. In COMP materials, equal emphasis in both speaking and writing assessment is given to rhetorical concerns (discourse or organization), psychological concerns (making contact with and attending to the perspective of the audience), and practical concerns (such as using vivid language and illustrations, to dramatize and create an effect). Little emphasis is given to formal errors such as mispronounced or misspelled words and pausing or punctuation, unless they noticeably detract from or obscure the message. These criteria are qualitatively scaled, to allow a norm-free judgment of the overall effect of a speech or essay. (p. 228)

Several other standardized tests appear to have potential for use in screening prospective or beginning teachers according to communication ability. McCaleb (1984) reports moderate correlations between two measures and the teaching performance of student teachers. The Snyder Speech Scale (Snyder, 1981) involves rating a prepared speech on a set of weighted criteria derived from pedagogical and communication literature. The Communication Competency Assessment Instrument (Rubin, 1983) includes a rating on a speech but also has a listening component and numerous interview-style questions related to other communication competencies such as giving directions and expressing empathy.

PERFORMANCE ASSESSMENT

In addition to standardized testing, nine states are estimating the competence of beginning teachers by observing and evaluating the teacher's classroom performance. Names of resource persons and documents from these states are given at the end of this chapter. Another 10 states are developing or exploring this option, which is called performance assessment.

Procedures among the nine states for performance assessment are quite diverse. This diversity creates special considerations for communication. Three variations are especially important.

1. The *definition* of variables. Some states write explicit definitions for each competency in order to focus upon particular behaviors. For its competency on using acceptable oral expression, Georgia gives four specific components: enunciation, delivery, usage, and pronunciation. Key points for these components are also given to further focus the observer on particular aspects of behavior. States that emphasize written definitions expect the observers to establish high levels of reliability before they observe teachers.

Other states give the observer more flexibility in defining variables. For example, Oklahoma also includes a competency on acceptable expression. The only direction given to the observer is a general reference to using correct grammar and appropriate vocabulary. In contrast with states such as Georgia, the observer has no additional guidance in interpreting "correct" and "appropriate."

2. The *focus* of the observer. In many performance assessments, the observer is directed to focus upon the teacher's behaviors with deliberate exclusion of students and any other persons interacting with the teacher. Sometimes the observer is directed to include attention to the learners' reactions to specific teacher's behaviors or to the teacher's use of students' ideas. The interactive quality seems to vary considerably across instruments.

3. The *role* of the observer. The most restricted role is for the observer to *tally* behaviors. Florida and Virginia have developed variations for this role. In Florida, the observer makes a frequency tabulation of precisely defined behavioral indicators each time they are demonstrated. For example, the observer makes a tally each time the teacher speaks too softly. Kentucky uses Florida's data collection system but adds a professional judgment by the observer.

11

Observers in Virginia mark coding sheets at seven-minute intervals to make a record of specific teaching behaviors. For example, when the teacher is questioning the students, the observer marks appropriate intersections in a matrix on the optical scan sheet. If the teacher asks a convergent question and rejects the student's answer, the block would be marked where these two categories converge as indicated by the X in the diagram below.

	Convergent Question	Divergent Question	Learner's Question
Teacher accepts	[ ]	[ ]	[ ]
Teacher rejects	[X]	[ ]	[ ]
Teacher redirects	[ ]	[ ]	[ ]
Teacher acknowledges	[ ]	[ ]	[ ]
Teacher praises	[ ]	[ ]	[ ]

The observer marks all such intersections that occur in the seven-minute period. An intersection would be marked only once during that time period even if the combination of behaviors was observed multiple times.

The major distinction of this role is the attempt to separate observation from judgment (Medley, Coker, & Soar, 1984). The observer records behaviors without knowing how these behaviors will be combined to yield a passing or failing score for the teacher on the competencies. Judgments about competencies are made by evaluators who use computer analysis of the recorded behaviors.

A second role has the observer search for a *match* between a set of written descriptions of teaching behaviors and the behaviors that are performed by the teacher. South Carolina has the observer decide whether the teacher demonstrates particular behaviors. For example, does the teacher communicate the instructional plan to students? After considering several ways that the plan may be communicated, the observer gives the teacher credit for demonstrating the competency and cites a specific instance or decides the plan was not communicated.

In using Georgia's instrument the observer decides how many behaviors from a set of four are demonstrated. For example, one indicator for the competency about communicating with learners is "gives explanations related to lesson content." The four descriptors are 1) explanations of lesson content are clear and easy to follow with appropriate vocabulary for learners; 2) communication is precise with few false starts, qualifiers, or interrupters; 3) demonstrations and/or examples are used to illustrate content; and 4) major points or potential areas of difficulty are emphasized using techniques such as repetition or verbal or nonverbal cues. Teachers are expected to demonstrate at least three of the four descriptors. Observers in North Carolina, Tennessee, and Texas also match behaviors with descriptions.

The third role for observers involves the preparation of a *narrative*. Oklahoma has implemented a narrative approach in which the observers take notes related to a general competency such as "effectively expresses self in written and verbal communication." Later the observers use their notes and other information to make a judgment regarding the status of the teacher on the competencies. South Dakota and Missouri are also moving toward the use of a narrative approach. (See Evertson & Green, 1986, for extensive discussion about using the narrative approach and for comparisons with other coding systems.)

Each variation among instruments—the focus and role of the observer and definition of variables—influences the quality of what is called "communication." For example, an exclusive focus upon the teacher imposes a linear model with characteristics of a sender of messages. Interactive or transactional models of communication (e.g., Trenholm, 1986) require the instrument to include all parties involved in the communication process.

Categories of Communication

While the states vary along the dimensions just described, they all have a list of competencies that can be analyzed for communication categories. Two reasons prompt a search for categories: to find which communication variables are considered important enough to be included in performance assessments, and to describe any differences in how these variables are defined.

Using the general procedures of content analysis (Borg & Gall, 1983; Bowers & Courtright, 1984), 12 communication categories were identified in competency lists prepared by the states. States that were using or considering performance assessments were asked for their competency lists and measures. (See the list of Documents and Contacts on Performance Assessment at the end of this chapter.) These lists were studied for explicit uses of the term "communication" or closely related words such as speaking, listening, and feedback. The analysis also attempted to identify other variables that relied heavily upon the communication process such as giving directions and questioning. The resulting categories were then used to classify the uses of communication within the competencies and measures. Representatives from states that prepared the measures agreed that the classification fairly represented the communication variables they considered to be in the competency lists.

The categories are listed in Table 2. Categories are generally organized beginning with the more precise and explicit behaviors and move toward those that are more diffused and more imprecisely defined. In discussing each category, at least one state practice is cited in detail. Significant variations in definition or measurement are also described.

13

Table 2. Communication Categories Drawn from Performance Assessments

Category	FL	GA	KY	NC	OK	SC	TN	TX	VA
1. Oral language usage (Correctness)		*			*	*	*	*	
2. Speech mechanics	*	*	*			*	*		
3. Fluency	*	*	*	*		*	*		
4. Feedback (monitors, praises)	*	*	*	*	*	*	*	*	*
5. Knowledge of subject matter		*				*	*	*	
6. Explaining	*	*	*	*	*	*	*	*	*
7. Enthusiasm and nonverbal communication	*	*	*		*	*			
8. Questioning	*	*	*	*		*		*	*
9. Directing	*	*	*		*	*		*	*
10. Emphasis	*	*	*					*	
11. Uses/elicits students' ideas		*				*	*	*	
12. Interactions with parents						*	*	**	

*Explicit reference to this category was found in the state's competency list or measure. In some cases where the category is unmarked, a state may incorporate the concept within another domain.
**Measurement of this competency is being developed.

Although the extent to which a category is used across the states is indicated, not all states with a competency within the category are discussed.

1. Oral Language Usage (Correctness)

Educators and others who have participated in developing competency lists for teachers often associate communication with correctness of language use. Almost all states include a competency with a focus on correctness. Interesting variations, however, can be detected in the ways states interpret and attempt to measure correctness.

At one extreme is the holistic, general-impression approach. All of Oklahoma's competencies tend to be more general than those of other states because its mode of data collection follows an open-ended, narrative approach. The wording of Oklahoma's competency illustrates the holistic method with the general phrase: "Effectively expresses self in written and verbal communication." The observer makes narrative notes concerning effective communication without being directed to specific behaviors. Oklahoma lists this competency as a "Professionalism" indicator.

Another example of the general-impression approach is found in Tennessee. Responsibility for the evaluation of beginning teachers rests with the local level; the state has more direct control over observation related to upper levels of the career ladder. Most districts use the state-developed observational system with explicit definition of competencies. The principal of beginning teachers also makes a holistic judgment about whether first-year teachers should be screened out of teaching on the basis of professionalism, writing ability, and correctness of oral communication. The intent is to retain teachers who provide an appropriate language model for students. The principal is urged to base the judgment about effective communication on four features: correct grammar usage, clear speech, organization of information, and vocabulary use that is appropriate to the level of the audience.

Other states use a more quantitative approach to evaluation and define explicitly acceptable grammar, usage, and vocabulary. One of the most specific guidelines for evaluating grammar is given by Texas. Located in Domain 3, Presentation of Subject Matter, is Criterion 8, Uses acceptable communication skills in presentation. One of the four performance indicators is "uses correct grammar," and the explanation for this indicator states: "Typical errors are 1) use of double negatives, 2) lack of subject-verb agreement, 3) incorrect verb tense, and 4) incorrect pronoun reference. Two or more errors are cause for denying credit." While the teacher might lose credit for a particular indicator, in the Texas evaluation system (as in other states where the observer "matches" behaviors with descriptions) the teacher could pass the criterion and, more importantly, pass the domain by scoring better on other indicators. Credit for the domain is necessary for continued certification; credit for each indicator is not essential.

Policies followed by states such as Georgia fall between the general and the specific approaches to correctness. Influenced by recommendations from the schools, Georgia increased attention to oral language in its 1985 revisions. A separate indicator was added for "Uses acceptable oral expression." Two of the four indicators concern correctness: one for oral language usage, the other for pronunciation. An indicator for written language usage precedes the one for oral usage and directs the observer to focus upon subject-verb agreement, verb tense, and pronoun reference. For oral expression, the key points for pronunciation focus on the production of specific words rather than the overall speech pattern. The intention is that the observer judge the students' understanding of the teacher's language. Georgia's evaluation system also does not require credit on each indicator. At least a minimal level of performance must be demonstrated on 75% or more of the indicators.

Texas elaborates further on the meaning of correct and clear pronunciation: "The teacher uses correct vowel/consonant/diphthong sounds and emphasizes correct syllables. Speech is free of slurring or mumbling of words."

15

Attempts to evaluate the correctness of language often evoke strong objections from advocates of linguistic diversity. Some assessment plans have been modified because of objections related to evaluating dialectal differences. Florida initially included assessment of correct usage but removed the items from its instrument because there was insufficient research evidence linking correct usage with effective teaching. An operating premise for the Florida Performance Measurement System is that only items with research support should be retained.

As described earlier, Tennessee's local implementation of the state guidelines requires the teacher's principal to decide whether the teacher should be screened out because of language use. South Carolina also makes an explicit reference to dialect in its performance assessment. The competency states, "Oral communication by the teacher is free of frequent errors in grammar." The explanation for the competency is, "The teacher's language does not contain *consistent errors* such as subject-verb disagreements. Spontaneous speech resulting in false starts or elaborate and embedded sentences are not considered errors. While accents or dialects are not considered here, *blatant mispronunciations unassociated with regional or group convention would deny credit. The absence of frequent or blatant errors* is sufficient evidence for demonstration."

Despite the problems related to dialect, most educators consider correctness of language use to be a critical attribute of effective communication. When competency lists are developed and submitted to educators for validation, the term "communication" seems to be most commonly associated with correct usage. In addition to the states listed above, many others (including Alabama, Arkansas, Connecticut, Maryland, and New Mexico) have competency lists indicating a relationship between effective communication and correct oral language use.

2. Speech Mechanics

Instruments used in performance assessment often list speech mechanics and correctness items together. Speech mechanics are vocal characteristics such as volume, rate, and pitch as well as articulation or enunciation. For example, Georgia's competency for acceptable oral expression has the two descriptors listed above for correctness and two descriptors for mechanics: 1) "enunciation makes speech understandable" and 2) "delivery (volume, rate of speaking, etc.) is suitable for the situation." Georgia's definition of enunciation is given in the key points: "Enunciation is the overall pattern of speech, sometimes called diction. Slurring, mumbling or other similar behaviors are symptoms of poor enunciation." The other descriptor concerns delivery and represents what most states emphasize in speech mechanics—volume and rate of speech. For example, Tennessee's guideline focuses attention on "speaks clearly at an appropriate pace and volume."

16

When observers judge speech mechanics, they usually focus on inadequacies in vocal qualities rather than on positive qualities. Florida is the most specific because the observer checks each occurrence of four behaviors: 1) loud, noisy, or grating voice; 2) shrill, piercing, highly pitched voice; 3) monotone—fails to vary the intensity, rate, and volume of speech; and 4) speaks too softly, almost inaudibly.

Rather than focusing on just the teacher, South Carolina instructs the observer to base the judgment on the observer's perception of the effect upon the learner. South Carolina's indicator focuses on potential negative effects also: "Speech and voice quality did not interfere with communication." Inadequate mechanics are indicated if the learners' concentration on the lesson is distracted by any interfering factor in the "volume, tone, characteristics, and speech mannerisms." The meaning of "characteristics" is not explained.

3. Fluency

A third category related to the oral language of teachers concerns speech fluency. North Carolina uses positive phrasing: "Teacher speaks fluently and precisely." Most other states refer to the negative qualities. Florida defines control of discourse as connected rather than scrambled and free from vagueness words. Examples of vague terms include sometimes, maybe, and probably. Georgia considers communication precise when there are few false starts, qualifiers, or interrupters. And in Texas, accurate language means the teacher does not overuse indefinite or vague terms.

Tennessee takes a broader perspective on fluency with an emphasis on "organized speech." The instructions state: "Mark this category when the teacher's spoken presentations demonstrate organization and coherence. Excessive rambling, jumping back and forth among topics or failure to organize points so that they demonstrate a logical flow of information will result in no check." Similarly, one of South Carolina's 11 criteria for acceptable communication is "a logical sequence is followed in the lesson."

4. Feedback (Monitors, Praises)

Educators seem to value the concept of "feedback" because the term is included on most competing lists. As might be expected, however, the use of the term varies. In some cases the concern is that the teacher be able to gather information (feedback) from the learners about their understanding. This is sometimes referred to as "monitoring." South Carolina distinguishes between monitoring and feedback. One of the criteria for "fulfilling instructional responsibilities" is to obtain information from students to determine the need for clarification, assistance, or adjustment. "This refers to *monitoring during the lesson* as opposed to a pretest." In

17

contrast, feedback concerns "the teacher's attempts to inform students of their accuracy or progress."

Monitoring is further specified in Tennessee's guidelines where the teacher "monitors learner understanding and reteaches as necessary." In Tennessee's instrument, monitoring includes identifying the learners' instructional levels before beginning instruction, pacing activities to accommodate learner differences, asking higher-order questions, and identifying misconceptions. Effective monitoring results in reteaching the material that learners do not understand.

Georgia also provides an interesting application of monitoring when the teacher anticipates misunderstandings. The competency is "Clarifies explanations when learners misunderstand lesson content." The four indicators are: 1) Areas of misunderstanding or difficulty are identified and communications are restated before learners ask questions, 2) Attempts are made to eliminate misunderstanding that occurs, 3) Different words or examples are used in clarifications, and 4) Clarifications are made for individuals or small groups rather than for the entire class or this type of clarification is not necessary.

Feedback is given special attention in North Carolina where: "1) Teacher provides feedback on the correctness or incorrectness of in-class work to encourage student growth; 2) Teacher regularly provides prompt feedback on assigned out-of-class work; 3) Teacher affirms a correct oral response appropriately, and moves on; 4) Teacher provides sustaining feedback after an incorrect response or no response by probing, repeating the question, giving a clue, or allowing more time."

Georgia also attends to this kind of feedback with an indicator on providing information to learners about their progress. The indicator includes stating the teacher's expectations about learners' outcomes, informing students when their performance is adequate or inadequate, and offering suggestions for improving performance.

Rather than giving a set of features, Texas presents the sequence of behaviors for effective feedback on student progress during instruction: 1) communicates learning expectations; 2) monitors students' performances as they engage in learning activities; 3) solicits responses or demonstrations from specific students for assessment purposes; 4) reinforces correct responses; 5) provides corrective feedback, or none needed; and 6) reteaches, or none needed. The scoring system, however, does not evaluate the total sequence but treats the steps as isolated items.

In contrast with the highly specified components of feedback, some instruments do not clarify dimensions but leave interpretation to the observer. For example, Oklahoma's competency states that the teacher "encourages class participation through interaction with students and feedback." Similarly, Missouri has the observer judge whether the teacher "is inconsistent in giving evaluative feedback" or "gives specific evaluative feedback." Since the instrument is not more explicit about what specific behaviors qualify as feedback, the observer has more latitude in interpreting classroom events.

Virginia indicates that teachers should "conduct recitation, to go over material students have studied on their own and make sure they have learned it." The observer records behaviors according to the categories on the observation form without judging the quality of feedback. The judgment about effectiveness of feedback is made through computer analysis of combinations of behaviors. The formula for combining behaviors is determined by the state department of education.

A few instruments isolate a particular type of feedback for special analysis. Florida emphasizes specific praise. Teachers should give specific academic praise rather than general, nonspecific praise. Teachers also should recognize students' responses, amplify, and give corrective feedback. They should not ignore the responses or react with sarcasm, disgust, or harshness.

Texas has similar indicators under the criterion for "Maintains supportive environment." For the indicator "Avoids sarcasm and negative criticism," the observer is advised: "Comments to or about learners which personally demean or embarrass them should be avoided. One occurrence is sufficient evidence for denying credit." South Carolina has a competency on the teacher's positive attitude with the criterion "methods are used to positively reinforce students who are engaged in learning."

5. *Knowledge of Subject Matter*

Many states make an explicit link between communication and subject matter knowledge. Georgia, South Carolina, and Texas all invoke the loss of credit for a competency if one significant error in content is made by the teacher. South Carolina's wording illustrates this in two competencies. The first states that the teacher's knowledge of subject matter is "communicated with confidence and authority." The other competency concerns the accuracy of information. One blatant error, noticeable to an out-of-field observer and uncorrected by the teacher, denies credit for the competency. In Tennessee, the teacher loses credit for a pattern of errors.

Elaboration of the relationship between communication and subject matter can be seen in Georgia's instrument. The third competency is "Demonstrates acceptable written and oral expression and knowledge of the subject." One of the four indicators states "demonstrates command of the school subject being taught" with these descriptors: 1) demonstrations and/or information presented to learners are accurate and up-to-date, 2) comments and responses to learner questions are accurate, 3) content is presented in a logical sequence, and 4) opportunity is provided for more than one level of learning.

19

Maryland's plan for assessing beginning teachers includes a descriptor under "shows command of subject matter" not found in other competency systems. The descriptor states: "Communicates information from a bias-free multicultural perspective."

6. *Explaining*

Explaining is usually identified as an essential competency for teachers, typically under an instructional domain rather than the communication domain. The importance of communication to teachers' explanations is shown in the narrative approach with the emphasis on clear presentation. Oklahoma describes the competency: "makes a clear and adequate explanation of material presented and procedures followed." Some instruments associate explaining with communication factors that have already been described. Georgia's four indicators for effective explaining are 1) use of emphasis, 2) vocabulary, 3) fluency, and 4) variety of examples. Indicators for effective explaining typically refer to the use of examples.

Several states provide more elaborate definitions of teachers' explanations. South Carolina calls for several features, including advance organizers, logical sequence, use of examples or demonstrations, and paraphrasing for clarification if needed. Virginia places explaining in the context of general instruction: "The teacher must be able to see that students have the learning experiences planned for them. The teacher must be able to: a. present material, to explain, define, demonstrate, etc." Sample behaviors that are combined for this competency include the teacher providing an answer to a learner's question, the teacher correcting a learner's error, and the teacher reviewing the lesson.

Tennessee includes providing a clear description of the learning task and its content as one indicator among the four for a teaching strategies competency. In addition to the components just described, Tennessee's instructions tell observers what to do when the teacher uses an indirect or discovery method of instruction: evaluate "in terms of the clarity to which students are led rather than the clarity of initial student responses." The observer is directed to focus on the teacher's behaviors rather than the learners'. Another feature is to give the lowest rating if any presentation of incorrect content or wrong information occurs regardless of the presentation's clarity.

The competency related to explaining behaviors also has been placed in special contexts. At least three states (Florida, Kentucky, and North Carolina) focus on the explanation of *concepts*. Florida and Kentucky add several items beyond the use of examples: "In presenting concepts the teacher is to use definitions, examples, attributes, and non-examples." Most states have items related to explaining that focus on giving the purpose of the lesson and directing students in their academic work.

20

As suggested in the Tennessee example, an interesting trend is to consider explanations as a test of the teacher's knowledge of subject matter. Texas incorporates "explains content and/or learning tasks clearly" within the domain for presentation of subject matter. The link between explaining/communicating and knowledge of subject matter is significant because one of the few items of near universal agreement about teaching is that the teacher should know the subject matter.

Knowledge of subject matter may be more complex than the representation given by most measures. As articulated in Shulman's (1986) recent research program, the ability to instruct a learner presupposes a knowledge of content that differs from the way a scholar of the discipline understands the content. Thus, scores on a standardized test representing the scholar's knowledge may not predict the ability to organize and interpret the content so that a learner can understand the information.

This ability to organize and interpret may be referred to as pedagogical content-knowledge. One test of the pedagogical content-knowledge appears to be the teacher's ability to communicate the content to a particular set of learners. Florida is attempting to develop instruments that measure pedagogical content-knowledge. These instruments would supplement the standardized, multiple-choice testing for knowledge of subject matter now used by most states.

7. Enthusiasm and Nonverbal Communication

More than half the states conducting performance assessments consider the communication of enthusiasm to be an essential teacher competency. Oklahoma simply asserts that teachers should exhibit enthusiasm for the subject matter without indicating how this might be done. Other states are more explicit with most citing nonverbal expressions as ways to demonstrate enthusiasm.

South Carolina elaborates that enthusiasm for learning and teaching is communicated when the teacher "demonstrates excitement, enjoyment, or animated involvement in learning through *intense or dramatic expression in gestures, movements, vocal inflections, or facial changes.*" Its directions to the observer continue: "It is not necessary to demonstrate enthusiasm throughout the period, but one example of *more than a momentary expression* must be cited for evidence. If demonstrated— Give a specific example of enthusiasm. If not demonstrated—State: 'No enthusiasm was demonstrated.'" South Carolina's experience in training observers shows that they most often award credit for *vocal* expressiveness.

Georgia's specification of "communicates personal enthusiasm" is similar as it includes facial expression, eye contact, voice inflection, energetic posture, and gestures. Georgia's key point to the observer goes

21

further and states that these nonverbal behaviors may be insufficient. The observer should monitor the learners to see if the teacher tends to inspire their attention and involvement. Florida contrasts the positive nonverbal behaviors with negative ones. The teacher should use body language that shows interest (smiling, gesturing, and steady eye contact) rather than lethargy (deadpan expressions and frowns).

Florida also looks for explicit verbal statements concerning enthusiasm. In a section labeled "task attraction and challenge," the observer notes teacher's behaviors that show "genuine zest for a task." The teacher also gets credit in this section for challenging the learners. For example, the teacher might make a zealous statement such as, "This next exercise is going to be fun; I know you will enjoy it."

8. Questioning

Performance assessments have not provided as much emphasis on teachers' questioning skills as might be expected from the attention in pedagogical literature. Perhaps the most extensive treatment is in Virginia, where the observer marks a number of questioning patterns such as teacher asks a convergent question, student makes a response, and teacher rejects the student's response. (This was illustrated earlier in the section on the roles of the observer.)

Sometimes questioning is included within a criterion that states the teacher should demonstrate a diversity of instructional methods. Georgia demonstrates this general concern for questioning with an evaluation of the teacher's assessment of learner progress during the lesson.

Florida and North Carolina isolate two features of questioning. Consistent with the training provided most preservice teachers, one feature is the use of several types of questions. Florida's observers record the frequency of questions. They also separate academic questions (including higher-order questions) from the nonacademic, procedural questions. North Carolina's competency focuses on appropriate levels of questions with a high rate of success. Both states also expect teachers to ask "single questions" so that the learner will not be confused. Florida states "Teacher asks direct questions one at a time without rephrasing or giving additional information."

South Carolina approaches competency with questioning in a more general way, from the learner's perspective. The competency states that questions meet the students' level of understanding.

9. Directing

Another competency that receives less attention in performance assessments than in literature on classroom management is giving directions. Sometimes directing is contained within a more general competency about effective classroom management. Observers in Oklahoma note in their narratives how well the teacher "gives clear, explicit directions to students."

Virginia's competency provides more explicit attention to giving clear directions: "Students understand what is expected of them. The teacher who knows this moves about during independent study and asks students if they need help." An example of a behavior related to this competency is when the observer records the teacher's making an oral assignment and giving step-by-step instructions.

One of Texas' five indicators for organizing materials and students is "gives clear administrative directions for classroom procedures or routines." The explanation for this indicator states: "The teacher communicates to the students what activities and/or tasks are to be done; when, where, and how the activities and/or tasks are to be done; and who will be involved in the activities and/or tasks." Texas as well as South Carolina and Georgia have a related competency for communicating expectations (rules) for student behavior.

10. Emphasis

As a subset of presenting information, several states recognize the importance of emphasizing particular points within the information. One of Georgia's indicators for effective explanations is that "major points or potential areas of difficulty are emphasized using techniques such as repetition or verbal or nonverbal cues." Texas elaborates: "The teacher uses strategies to emphasize to the students the structure of the content. For example, the teacher uses voice inflection, underlines important points, repeats points for emphasis, explains relationships. If instruction proceeds without some points standing out, important dimensions have not been adequately specified." In Florida, observers note the frequency of "marker expressions, marker techniques, and repetition." To receive credit for this competency, the teacher tells students explicitly that specific information is important and repeats or restates the important points.

11. Uses/Elicits Students' Ideas

Another skill receiving attention in a few states concerns the teacher's ability to encourage students to communicate their ideas. Georgia focuses upon this dimension more than others through the competency "uses learner responses or questions regarding lesson content." The descriptors are: 1) Comments, questions, examples, demonstrations or other contributions are *sought* from learners throughout the lesson; 2) Learners who wish to comment or to seek assistance are recognized or no learners seek recognition; 3) Learner responses, ideas, questions, or other contributions are acknowledged; and 4) Learners' ideas are elaborated in the lesson through teacher comments, questions and/or extended wait time. Other states, including Oklahoma and South Carolina, also affirm the importance of teachers encouraging students to express their ideas.

A related competency concerns the teacher's ability to engage the students in discussion. Two of Missouri's 19 competencies focus on communication. One, already mentioned, concerns feedback; the other is difficult to classify because of its generality: "demonstrates ability to communicate effectively with students." The guideline for a satisfactory rating seems to place it within this category as the teacher is expected to "encourage relevant dialogue" with students.

An interesting variation on the teacher's ability to promote the communications of learners is Connecticut's concern for fostering the independence of the student as a learner. Teachers can facilitate independence by probing with questions that stimulate students to recall, analyze, synthesize, and evaluate. Connecticut's document also asserts that teachers can express an expectation for independent learning.

12. Interacting With Parents

In addition to communicating effectively with learners, teachers are often expected to interact positively with parents. This competency is often stated in initial plans for competency assessment, but it is sometimes minimized as the emphasis focuses upon classroom observation. For example, Georgia includes communicating with parents in an optional instrument on professional standards.

Oklahoma has retained this competency, perhaps because its narrative approach allows data collection outside the classroom. The competency states that the teacher interacts and communicates effectively with parents and staff. Similarly, Tennessee's descriptive approach to gathering data about beginning teachers includes an item related to communication with parents. The competency, "reports learner status and progress to learners and their parents," has these descriptors: "explains grading standards to students and parents; keeps accurate records of student progress; submits report cards on required timelines; holds conferences with parents."

Texas is in the process of implementing a performance assessment that includes a criterion "interacts and communicates effectively with parents." Indicators of this criterion document certain behaviors: 1) initiates communications with parents about student performance and/or behavior when appropriate, 2) conducts parent-teacher conferences in accordance with local district policy, 3) reports student progress to parents in accordance with local district policy, and 4) maintains confidentiality unless disclosure is required by law.

24

Plans for performance assessment often begin with more extensive attention to teacher-parent communications. For example, Connecticut's list of competencies includes "Encourages and maintains the cooperative involvement and support of parents and the community." Indicators for this competency include: 1) establishes ongoing two-way communication with parents based on mutual respect, 2) obtains and uses information about students from parents, 3) communicates goals and objectives for both program and student to parents, and 4) conducts effective parent/teacher conferences. Although procedures for assessing other competencies have been developed, Connecticut has not yet implemented this competency.

Summary

All the states reviewed in this chapter have asserted the importance of teacher communications in their competency lists and performance measures. Twelve categories have emerged. The categories represent the prevailing perceptions of those communication dimensions that are important and/or measurable. They also sketch the parameters of understanding. For example, speech mechanics can be precisely defined but are not uniformly considered essential. The concept of feedback is valued by all, and rather precise components of monitoring are specified. Communication as an index to the teacher's knowledge of content is an exciting frontier.

Overall, the emphasis has been upon characteristics of the teacher as a speaker. Nine of the dimensions (correctness, mechanics, fluency, knowledge of subject matter, explaining, enthusiasm, questioning, directing, and emphasis) focus on the teacher with limited or no attention to any other party in the communication.

Much less attention has been given to communication as a dynamic, interactive process than to the linear, one-way flow of information. A problem may be exhibited in the tension between a dynamic concept and the restrictions imposed by particular systems of measurement. The dimensions of feedback, use of student ideas, and communicating with parents generally reflect the process approach to communication. In some instruments other dimensions also look beyond isolated teacher behaviors. For example, questioning sometimes includes attention to rate of success or adjustment to the level of the learner, and teachers' enthusiasm can be related to pupils' interest. The more recent attempts to focus on the communication of the teacher's understanding of subject matter begin to look at an exchange of meaning rather than the sending of messages.

This analysis of how states are assessing teachers' communications provides a useful map of our practical understanding of instructional communication. In order to advance this understanding, theoretical models of communication need to be considered. Consulting research on teaching and communication also can promote our understanding of teachers' communications. Building a better understanding of communication promotes the advancement of assessment and development of effective teaching.

DOCUMENTS AND CONTACTS ON
PERFORMANCE ASSESSMENT

Connecticut State Department of Education. (1984). Connecticut Teaching Competencies in *Standards and Procedures for Approval of Teacher Preparation Programs*. Gail Tomala, Office of Research and Evaluation, Connecticut State Department of Education, Box 2219, Hartford, CT, 06145.

Florida State Department of Education. (1983 revision). *Florida Performance Measurement System*. Garfield Wilson or Betty Fry, Teacher Education and Certification, Department of Education, Collins Building, Tallahassee, FL, 32301.

Georgia State Department of Education. (1985 revision). *Teacher Performance Assessment Instruments*. Lester Solomon, Teacher Education and Certification, Georgia State Department of Education, Twin Towers East, Atlanta, GA, 30334.

Kentucky Department of Education. (1985). *Testing and Internship*. Dorothy Archer, Teacher Testing/Internship Program, Division of Teacher Education and Certification, Kentucky Department of Education, Frankfort, KY, 40601.

Maryland State Department of Education. (1986). *Maryland Beginning Teacher Program: An Overview*. Louise Tanney, Division of Certification and Accreditation, Maryland State Department of Education, 200 W. Baltimore St., Baltimore, MD, 21210.

Missouri Department of Elementary and Secondary Education. (1984). *Guidelines for Performance Based Teacher Evaluation*. Turner Tyson, Teacher Education and Certification, Missouri Department of Elementary and Secondary Education, Box 480, Jefferson City, MO, 65102.

North Carolina State Department of Public Instruction. (1985). *North Carolina Initial Certification Program*. Ione Perry, Division of Program Approval, North Carolina State Department of Public Instruction, Raleigh, NC, 27611.

Oklahoma State Department of Education. (1985). *Oklahoma Entry-Year Assistance Program*. Joseph Weaver, Teacher Education/Testing/Staff Development, Oklahoma State Department of Education, Oklahoma City, OK 73105-4599.

South Carolina State Department of Education. (1986 revision). *Assessments of Performance in Teaching*. Kathy Thomas, Teacher Assessment Unit, Office of Research, South Carolina Department of Education, 1429 Senate Street, Room 603, Columbia, SC, 29201.

South Dakota Department of Education and Cultural Affairs. (1986). *First Year Assistance Report*. Diane Alexander, Certification Office, South Dakota Department of Education and Cultural Affairs, Kneip Bldg, 700 N. Illinois St., Pierre, SD, 57501-2293.

Tennessee State Department of Education. (1985–1986). *State Model for Local Evaluation.* George Malo, Teacher Education & Certification, Tennessee Department of Education, 111 Cordell Hull Bldg, Nashville, TN, 37219-5338.

Texas Education Agency. (1986). *Texas Teacher Appraisal System. Teacher Orientation Manual.* Susan Barnes, Division of Teacher Education, Texas Education Agency, 1701 N. Congress, Austin, TX, 78701.

Virginia Department of Education. Nancy Vance, Personnel and Professional Development, Virginia Department of Education, P.O. Box 6Q, Richmond, VA, 23216.

References

Borg, W. R., & Gall, M. D. (1983). *Educational research: An introduction* (4th ed.). New York: Longman.

Bowers, J. W., & Courtright, J. A. (1984). *Communication research methods.* Glenview, IL: Scott, Foresman, & Co.

Carnegie Forum on Education and the Economy. (1986). *A nation prepared: Teachers for the 21st century.* New York: Carnegie Corporation.

Educational Testing Service. (1984). *A guide to the NTE core battery tests.* Princeton, NJ: Author.

Evertson, C., & Green, J. (1986). Observation as inquiry and method. In M. C. Wittrock (Ed.), *Handbook of research on teaching,* (3rd ed.) (pp. 162–213). New York: Macmillan.

Holmes Group, (1986). *Tomorrow's teachers: A report of the Holmes Group,* East Lansing, MI: Author.

Joekel, R. (1986). Tracking the reform movement. *News, notes, and quotes, 31,* (2), 1.

McCaleb, J. L. (1984). Selecting a measure of oral communication as a predictor of teaching performance. *Journal of Teacher Education, 35* (5), 33–38.

Medley, D. M., Coker, H., & Soar, R. S. (1984). *Measurement-based evaluation of teacher performance.* New York: Longman.

National Governors' Association. (1986). *Time for results: The governors' 1991 report on education.* Washington, DC: Author.

Ortman, P. E., & Tanney, L. (1986). *Beginning teacher performance evaluation programs: A state by state survey.* Unpublished manuscript: Maryland State Department of Education.

Roth, R. A., & Mastain, R. (Eds.). (1984). *The NASDTEC manual on certification and preparation of educational personnel in the United States.* Sacramento, CA: National Association of State Directors of Teacher Education and Certification.

Rubin, R. B. (1983). *The communication competency assessment instrument.* Falls Church, VA: Speech Communication Association.

Shulman, L. S. (1986). Paradigms and research programs in the study of teaching: A contemporary perspective. In M. C. Wittrock (Ed.), *Handbook of research on teaching,* (3rd ed.) (pp. 3–36). New York: Macmillan.

Snyder, S. L. (1981). *An investigation to develop and validate a rating scale for the assessment of the speaking competence of preservice teachers.* Unpublished doctoral dissertation, The Pennsylvania State University.

Trank, D. M., & Steele, J. M. (1983). Measurable effects of a communication skills course: An initial study. *Communication Education, 32* (2), 227–236.

Trenholm, S. (1986). *Human communication theory.* Englewood Cliffs, NJ: Prentice-Hall.

2

The Communication Skills Of Teachers: A Coherent Conception

Jerry D. Feezel

Kent State University

Y ears ago when I was a novice high school teacher I remember being asked by a seasoned veteran, "Do you teach kids or do you teach speech?" Actually he was only half-seriously testing me with that question, which even then I realized as an unfair dilemma. It is encouraging to note from chapter 1 that there are attempts at testing teachers more fairly with the recognition that teaching involves both aspects of the question—that is, communicating subject knowledge to "kids."

Skill in communication is central to effective teaching. Hurt, Scott, and McCroskey (1978) once suggested that communication was the difference between knowing and teaching. Knowing your subject field plus principles and strategies of teaching is only part of the task; being able to teach what you know requires the application of communication skills. Many studies have demonstrated the relationship between a teacher's communication and successful classroom instruction (Daly & Korinek, 1980; Feezel & Rubin, 1983; Rubin & Feezel, 1986). Therefore, the assessment of how well teachers communicate may be central to the improvement of their teaching effectiveness. Those assessments must be designed and implemented, however, according to a valid and coherent conception of the complex process of communication in instruction. Otherwise, the judgments of a teacher's communication may be based on ill-conceived, inaccurate understandings of process; isolated discrete factors that may be insignificant; or piecemeal measurements without a unifying principle.

The purpose of this chapter is to review conceptions of the field of communication generally, with particular application to the speech communication of teachers. Because many states are involved in the national trend toward teacher testing, as McCaleb noted in chapter 1, there is the danger that these efforts will not always follow conceptions that fit the realities of teaching. The varied and sometimes superficial approaches to communication assessment across the states raise the dangerous possibility of judgments based upon an incomplete or fragmented picture of a teacher's communication skills. For example, McCaleb noted in chapter 1 that 9 of the 12 communication dimensions assessed by states focus on specific factors of the teacher without considering the dynamics of the teacher interacting with others. Throughout the chapter we see that certain state assessment practices may focus on discrete, isolated mechanics of communication rather than a carefully integrated holistic assessment based upon a soundly conceived view of communication instruction. Therefore, this chapter draws from current concepts in the field and previous research findings to synthesize a holistic conception of the teacher communication process.

The field of communication has been in existence since the time of Isocrates, one of the first teachers of speech in Athens during the fifth century B.C. The primary role of Isocrates and other teachers after him was to develop skilled speakers to participate in the democratic governance of the city states. His students were taught to prepare, memorize, and declaim somewhat formal speeches in the assemblies and courts. The Greek society was centered in oral discourse, with all citizens expected to actively participate by arguing their views on issues. Thus rhetoric, as the focal point of all education, was the art of persuasive discourse— especially through logic or argument. Just as education today has expanded considerably, so too, has speech education and the role of communication in instruction. Although a focus on persuasion and argument remains, much of teacher communication involves other roles and functions such as explaining information or orally interpreting an author's words.

The breadth and variety of communicative functions were reviewed by the Speech Communication Association (SCA) National Project on Speech Communication Competencies (Allen & Brown, 1976). Three years of research and development led to several conclusions, including a definition of communication competence and a functional approach. Competence involves a repertoire of experiences or strategies from which one selects, implements, and evaluates the communicative performance. Although these dimensions of competence were developed as applicable to all communication, they seem especially fitting to teacher communication. The repertoire involves what is known of subject and pedagogy, but teaching constitutes selecting, implementing, and evaluating what is done.

The national project developed a functional approach to competence that is broader than the persuasive focus of ancient times. In addition to communication that functions to control or influence others, we may use communication to inform, express feelings, imagine, or perform social rituals (Allen & Brown, 1976).

1. Ritualizing. These are the everyday social graces of greetings, turntaking, raising hands, and other such means of regulating the formalities required by the situation.
2. Informing. The purpose is primarily to give or seek information, data, ideas, or knowledge. This function probably occupies most of the time-on-task in teaching.
3. Controlling. The intent is persuading or attempts to influence the ideas, behavior, or feelings of others.
4. Expressing Feelings. Although feelings may be involved in the other functions, the primary purpose here is expressing attitudes or emotions without trying to influence; the focus is self-expression or disclosure of affective states.
5. Imagining. This usually involves aesthetic activities for creativity, roleplaying, exploring hypothetical instances, or fantasizing. The purpose may be to entertain or to envision or predict the future.

These five functions recognize more fully the numerous purposes served by communication. Much of the classroom role of teaching involves the informing process, whether explaining through lectures or seeking information through questions and discussions. Other aspects of teacher communication employ professional and social rituals, using or encouraging imagination, relating to feelings, and communicating to control a situation. Any assessments of communication in instruction must recognize the breadth of functions served and integrate them into a view of the total process. The prominence of these five functions articulated by the national project is evident from their use in nearly 30 publications on instructional communication, including articles, books, curriculum guides, and assessment standards.

We can see that the study of oral communication has undergone considerable development from its roots in ancient rhetoric to the taxonomy of speech communication developed by another SCA national committee (McBath & Jeffrey, 1978). Its description of the contemporary field begins with a definition of speech communication as a study of "the nature, processes, and effects of human symbolic interaction" (p. 187). Any situation or context where humans are using language along with nonverbal codes (e.g., body movements, facial expressions, distances, etc.) to send and receive messages may be examined by communication assessments. Just as our world is more complex today than in ancient Greece, so too is speech communication a much broader and more complex endeavor than simply speechmaking. Such breadth is evident in the following major categories of the McBath and Jeffrey taxonomy (1978, pp. 187–188).

Code Systems: verbal and nonverbal
Intercultural Communication, across ethnic backgrounds
Interpersonal Communication: person-to-person and groups
Organizational Communication within formal systems
Oral Interpretation of literature through performance
Pragmatic Communication to influence or aid decisions
Public Address: speakers, campaigns, and movements
Rhetorical and Communication Theory to explain behaviors
Speech and Hearing Science: physiological and acoustical

These categories of research and development in speech communication show the complexity of the total process that must be considered in any coherent conception of teacher communication assessment. They also constitute subdivisions of the field wherein considerable research and expertise exist. (Further information about the taxonomy is available from the SCA, 5105 Backlick Road, Annandale, VA 22003.)

Speech Communication Education, another category of the McBath and Jeffrey (1978) taxonomy, is the focal area for this monograph and the conception of teacher communication skills in the remainder of this chapter. Subdivisions within the category are (1) Communication Development, acquisition and use of skills by normal children; (2) Oral Communication Skills, improving individual competencies in speaking and listening; and (3) Instructional Communication, communicative factors involved in the teaching-learning process.

The third subdivision, instructional communication, has been the subject of much contemporary research on the oral communication competencies that all teachers must attain. An overview of some major areas of that research will show the skills that must be encompassed by a complete conception of teacher speech communication. The intent here is not to provide a complete review of research findings but rather to identify the types and functions of teacher communication to be included in a holistic assessment.

RESEARCH ON TEACHER COMMUNICATION

The SCA and the American Theatre Association (ATA) prepared a set of competency models for elementary and secondary teachers (SCA/ATA Joint Task Force on Teacher Preparation, 1978). The skills identified for teachers in all content areas were grouped into six main competency areas: (1) preparation of messages appropriate to various audiences and purposes; (2) delivering messages appropriate to various contexts; (3) analyzing and managing factors in communication processes; (4) demonstrating effective listening skills in a variety of contexts; (5) demonstrating values that promote communication processes and artistic experiences appropriate to a multicultural, democratic society; and (6) recognizing the role of mass communication in American society. These were further reduced to specific skills and behaviors. For example, under delivering messages appropriate to various contexts, one skill area was "demonstrating the appropriate use of verbal and non-verbal language by":

1. delivering messages for a variety of communication purposes and audiences,
2. demonstrating a sense of drama in storytelling or reading aloud,
3. enhancing listener comprehension and interest through facial and bodily expressions that are congruent with meanings,
4. demonstrating enthusiasm in relating with others.

These are simply examples of the specific kinds of statements that may make appropriate standards for assessment. It appears from chapter 1 that not all state assessment procedures have reached this level of specificity in criteria, nor have they all attended to the complete sets of standards contained in the SCA/ATA document. Yet all six competency areas seem important to an assessment of the total competence of an instructor and should be included in a complete conception of instructional communication.

Another paradigm (Lynn, 1976) concisely grouped communication skills into two categories, message-sending and message-receiving. The message-sending skills included:

1. analyzing students to determine initial guidelines for message construction—most suitable presentation channels, most engaging delivery techniques, etc.;
2. selecting, organizing, supporting, and clearly expressing ideas in a verbal and nonverbal manner appropriate to the students, e.g, giving directions, lecturing, explaining, questioning, stimulating discussion; and
3. using numerous ways to solicit feedback, express approval or disapproval, and criticize or evaluate student communication.

The basic message-receiving skills for teachers were:

1. identifying central ideas and supporting arguments;
2. weighing evidence and reasoning;
3. listening for different levels of meaning in messages;
4. listening and responding with empathic sensitivity; and
5. interpreting nonverbal messages.

Together, Lynn's (1976) categories reflect an important balance in attention to the two-way process of communication that must be recognized in a coherent conception of instructional communication. In addition, the skills listed above identify many specific areas of research conducted after she categorized competencies.

Communication and education research during the past 10 years has identified trends in communication variables thought to be important in teacher assessment (Feezel & Rubin, 1983; Rubin & Feezel, 1985; Staton-Spicer & Wulff, 1984). There are five focus areas in recent teacher communication research—lectures, verbal communication, questioning skills, nonverbal communication, and interpersonal relations—that indicate how assessment might be conceptually grounded. These research clusters may also be compared with the 12 state assessment dimensions identified in chapter 1.

Lectures. Weaver and Michel (1983) list many studies that include such variables as mediated lectures (e.g., videotape or film), mass lectures, organization, nonverbal code use, and training teaching assistants. This topic area, which is like formal public speaking with its traditional treatment of informing and persuading, is central to instructional communication. In terms of the assessment trends noted by McCaleb in chapter 1, at least 6 of the 12 dimensions used seem to pertain directly to lecturing (correctness, mechanics, fluency, knowledge of subject, explaining, and emphasis).

Factors such as limited attention spans of learners, demands for variety and excitement (to compete with television's pace or visual appeal), and bad lecturing practices, however, have led to the need for using alternatives to lectures. Innovative approaches include discussions, games, simulations, small groups, independent study, and field projects. This trend shifted classroom communication research emphasis to a broader examination of teachers' verbal and nonverbal skills.

Verbal communication. A second rather general and eclectic research cluster is frequently indexed as "teacher verbal behavior" in the *Education Index*. This label encompasses much research on several variables of teachers' verbal communication, not simply lecturing. Variables examined include praise, attention, approval, and feedback. Some of these topics have been given considerable attention (Brophy, 1981). In contrast, a teacher's use of humor is another interesting research line that has received only slight attention. Bryant (1979) identified patterns of humor in college teachers that may have influence on learning. Both research areas have stressed a functional approach like Allen & Brown (1976). It appears that humor and praise can be integrated with several of the five functions, depending upon context, showing the importance of a holistic integration of communication factors in teaching assessment.

Teacher clarity has been another major, promising line of research focus during the past few years (e.g., Land, 1981; McCaleb, 1984). McCaleb and Rosenthal (1984) noted that patterns of explanations, vagueness terms, vocal hesitations, and checking for understanding have potential for positive influence on both student achievement and perceptions. This is an ongoing research topic that is central to much of teaching and relates most closely to the informing function. Language variables in teacher verbalization have received attention in the areas of ethnicity and sexism, but other factors such as language intensity or probability words have been largely neglected.

Extensive research has been done in sociolinguistics, or language and social class, and in the general area of classroom interaction. Findings have not been included here because of the monograph's focus on assessing teachers' communication rather than the learners'.

Attention given to language and verbalization in research is mixed, with some topics, such as clarity and praise, examined more than others. Explaining was one of the 12 focal dimensions deemed central to teaching in the state assessments. Yet the place of language in verbal assessment seems to be largely that of correctness and fluency with scant attention given to more interactive process factors such as humor and language interpretations by learners. Generally, both the research and assessment practices have concentrated on the teacher's precision with little attention to the dynamics of interaction with students in the instructional uses of language. But the findings of many studies on humor, clarity, praise, feedback, and ethnicity often have implied that the assessment of a teacher's use of language must rely on individual learner factors. This suggests that analysis of learning contexts and the dynamics of shared meanings must be central to a conception of communication in instruction.

Questioning skills. Questioning overlaps the verbal cluster, but is treated separately because research focused on this area has been conducted and indexed independently from the above categories. Much research has focused on the questions teachers use. One review of published "teacher talk" research in the last five years revealed more than 25 studies with variables such as types and levels of questions, phrasing, probes, response duration, wait time, and leading discussions (Feezel & Faix, 1983). Still, much remains to be learned about questioning behavior. For example, a major researcher in this area found only half the responses of high school students were on the same cognitive level as the teacher's question (Dillon, 1982). This finding and the conflicting findings of several studies on the efficacy of higher order questions represent at least two points for further research.

Nonverbal communication. Smith (1979) presents an extensive and detailed review of almost 250 articles and books about environment,

35

space, body movement, facial expression, eye use, physical appearances, objects/apparel, and vocal cues. From this, Smith concludes that vocal cues and silence are neglected variables in research on teaching. Although Stern (1980) discussed the teacher's voice in relation to acting and Anderson and Withrow (1981) studied the effect of nonverbal expressiveness, little research on vocal cues has been done since 1979.

Nonverbal communication is especially important because of its relationship to expressing feelings. Many state assessment procedures emphasize the expression of enthusiasm nonverbally. The neglect of research into vocal cues in teaching contrasts with the stress on voice mechanics in many state systems. Perhaps research on voice in teaching would reveal whether such importance is warranted. Few workable systems for analyzing nonverbal codes in teaching have been developed and widely used. Only two systems integrate the nonverbal with verbal categories for a more complete communication analysis (see Galloway in Simon & Boyer, 1967, and Cambra's VAN system in Feezel, 1983). Further research could test these systems and work toward a theoretical synthesis of verbal and nonverbal skills in teaching.

Interpersonal Relations. This cluster of variables includes several studies that focus on interpersonal skills and relationships. Factors such as teacher warmth, openness, self-disclosure, supportive/defensive climate, listening with empathy, and interpersonal solidarity have been examined in research efforts (e.g., Boser & Poppen, 1978; Rosenfeld, 1983; Wasserman, 1982). Interpersonal relationship factors may be associated more with learner attitudes and motivation or affective learning than with the learning of objective content. This suggests an association with the functions of feeling, ritualizing, and controlling more than informing.

State assessments reviewed in chapter 1 also touch upon this category only occasionally in relation to the interactive dimensions of feedback, use of student ideas, and interactions with parents. Nevertheless, the importance of this cluster frequently is stressed in student perceptions and underlined by expert opinions. Interpersonal research has been conducted in many disciplines, but it represents a major area of contemporary study in speech communication with numerous scholarly contributions, including direct applications to instructional communication (Feezel, 1983).

From this review of the research areas in instructional communication, it seems that Allen and Brown's (1976) five functions have been differentially treated. Variables relative to informing, controlling, and expressing feelings have been researched more than the others. The ritualizing function may have been examined slightly in indirect ways but not as a focal point. Similarly, the teacher's use of imagining for creative or predictive activities has been the least researched topic area in speech communication. Yet all five functions are viable and relevant to communication in the instruction of any subject, though the prevalence of some may vary with the subject matter. An implication of this review, then, is the need for further research pertaining to ritualizing and imagining functions.

The five clusters of instructional communication research reviewed above indicate the factors that have been identified as significant to effective teaching. The results and conclusions of the research may be consulted for detailed guidelines, but this overview suggests the elements that must be considered for a complete, coherent process approach to communication skill assessment of teachers.

One issue raised by the studies and theoretical perspectives in instructional communication is how to organize our knowledge of teacher communication skills into a coherent conception. Communication theorists have often attempted to forge comprehensive models of this complex process, but no single conception has been definitive. Some contemporary theorists have indicated, however, that any model of human communication must recognize the complex, ongoing, and simultaneous nature of the cue-exchanging process involving two or more individuals. Although earlier communication models have viewed the process as an interaction with messages being sent back and forth between two people much like a tennis match, the concept of a transaction seems more accurate. As McCaleb noted at the end of chapter 1, we should view teacher communication as an "exchange of meaning rather than just the sending of messages" (p. 25). The concept recognizes that when two or more people are face-to-face, perception and reaction to cues are constant and simultaneous.

It is more accurate to say that we adjust and change our messages midstream based on the totality of reactions we observe or hear from our listeners. Even in the tennis analogy, good players do not simply wait idly for the ball to be in their court. They constantly adapt to the strategies and moves of the opponent. The communication process is not one of "I speak–now you speak–then I speak–then you ..." but is a mutual and continuous exchanging of verbally and nonverbally coded ideas, feelings, etc.

This transactional perspective has been attempted in several contemporary models (e.g., Barnlund, 1970; Bois, 1978; Feezel, 1983; Harris, 1967). All are generalized models of communication, though, and not applied to the nature of educational communication situations. The classroom is a similarly complex transactive process of communication. Therefore, the instructional communication conception that follows is an attempt to synthesize the numerous factors studied in research into a transactional model of teacher communication. This conception may then be used to guide assessment efforts to help assure that valid, holistic judgments are made about teacher communication skills.

37

A COHERENT CONCEPTION OF TEACHER COMMUNICATION

The process of speaking and listening within the role of "teacher" is best conceptualized in terms of an ordered set of five skill areas that constitute the ABCDEs of instructional communication. Each competency or skill identified in the previous research overview can be located within one or more of the five phases. These are sequential steps only in the sense of beginning with A and progressing to D or E for an initial situation or episode. Otherwise these are not linear steps but a constantly iterative process of interwoven factors or phases. Throughout a situation or communicative interchange the participants would be constantly cycling through the five skill areas.

A. Analyzing the situation. The teacher needs to be skilled in noticing, identifying, and interpreting the varieties of situational codes and cues. For example, Lynn's (1976) initial message-sending category of "analyzing students to determine initial guidelines for message construction" is incorporated here. This phase is important for the initial "understanding" of the people and the setting, but continues throughout the occasion as teachers constantly note and adjust to their perceptions of cues. The interpretation of both verbal and nonverbal cues would be important skills here, and the application of rhetorical and communication theory from the McBath and Jeffrey (1978) taxonomy would be central to this phase.

B. Being willing to communicate. The teacher must have the internal strength and motivation to communicate as required by analysis of the situation. This could involve such factors as self-confidence, low apprehension or reticence, willingness to get involved with others, and assertiveness to exert rights to influence or control students. The relevance and assessment of such factors are noted in Rubin and Feezel (1986). A willingness to appropriately self-disclose could also be a factor in this general area. Thus some of the research into interpersonal relations reviewed earlier could pertain to this phase as well as Phase C below. All these factors have been regarded as skills amenable to assessment and development.

C. Creating a climate for persons. Teachers must build interpersonal relationships with students, staff, parents, etc., because such behavior is important to their effectiveness. This means fostering communication "between persons" to set positive conditions for the actual communication transactions. "Demonstrating enthusiasm in relating with others" (SCA/ATA Joint Task Force, 1978) fits here as a way to foster a healthy transactional climate. Remember, some of the state assessments emphasized teacher enthusiasm and nonverbal communication as an important

38

dimension. Generally, the research into nonverbal codes and interpersonal relations would enlighten assessments in this phase especially.

The next two component areas of the model (D and E) deal with the situations and types of interchanges that occur in education. Depending on who is involved at the moment, areas D and E would be involved alternatively.

D. During-class instructional transactions. These are the complex interchanges of teacher and student that teachers must master. Skills herein pertain to the interplay of the modes of communication with the five functions of the transaction (Allen & Brown, 1976). The functions are the purposes of the specific instances of communication, the needs or intentions served. Although it is a rather distinct type, an instance could involve mixed functions. The modes refer to the particular nature of the speaking-listening activity occurring in the classroom (e.g., number involved and with how much interchanging of speaking roles). The modes tend to be presentational in focus (the teacher doing most of the talking) or more interactive in nature as in group or class interchanges. The modes of presenting focus on teacher-to-individual or teacher-to-class uses of lecturing, giving directions, explaining, and orally interpreting materials. The interacting modes involve competencies from the research such as using questions, leading discussions, listening skills, feedback, and praise, with one student or an entire class.

E. Extra-class transactions. These occur with (1) peers (fellow teachers in departments, committees, etc.); (2) professionals (in associations and conferences); (3) powers (principals, superintendents, etc.); and (4) parents (or guardians of students). Transactions with parents were considered important in some of the state assessments reviewed by McCaleb. As in area D, one or more of the five functions would also pertain to the interchanges with these other parties.

Other communication competencies reviewed in the first section of this chapter may also fit into the model. For example, all the skills identified by the SCA/ATA Joint Task Force (1978) could be located in the relevant components of the teacher communication model. As an example, "demonstrating a sense of drama in story telling or reading aloud" clearly fits in category D, class presentations.

Whatever set (or sets) of guidelines are used for the assessment of teacher communication, a coherent, organized conceptual model should be used to assure a valid holistic assessment. Since many states are involved in the national trend toward teacher testing, there is the danger that these efforts will not always follow conceptions that fit the realities of teaching. Equally dangerous is the possibility of assessments that yield an incomplete or fragmented picture of an individual teacher's communication skills. It has been the intent of this chapter to help guard against such pitfalls by providing an overview of the domain of speech communication in teaching and by synthesizing a coherent, holistic conception of teacher communication transactions.

References

Allen, R. R., & Brown, K. L. (Eds.). (1976). *Developing communication competence in children.* Skokie, IL: National Textbook.

Anderson, J. F., & Withrow, J. G. (1981). The impact of lecturer nonverbal expressiveness on improving mediated instruction. *Communication Education, 30,* 342–353.

Barnlund, D. C. (1970). A transactional model of communication. In K. K. Sereno & C. D. Mortensen. (Eds.), *Foundations of communication theory* (pp. 83–102). New York: Harper & Row.

Bois, J. S. (1978). *The art of awareness* (3rd ed.). Dubuque, IA: Brown.

Boser, J., & Poppen, W. A. (1978). Identification of teacher verbal response roles for improving student-teacher relationships. *Journal of Educational Research, 72,* 90–93.

Brophy, J. (1981). Teacher praise: A functional analysis. *Review of Educational Research, 51,* 5–32.

Bryant, J., Gula, J. M., & Zillman, D. (1979). Teachers' humor in the college classroom. *Communication Education, 29,* 110–118.

Daly, J. A., & Korinek, J. T. (1980). Instructional communication theory and research: An overview of classroom interaction. In D. Nimmo (Ed.), *Communication Yearbook 4* (pp. 515–532). New Brunswick, NJ: Transaction.

Dillon, J. T. (1982). Cognitive correspondence between question-statement and response. *American Educational Research Journal, 19,* 540–551.

Feezel, J. D. (1983). *Between persons: On becoming an interpersonal communicator in teaching.* Dubuque, IA: Gorsuch-Scarisbrick.

Feezel, J. D., & Faix, N. M. (1983). *Teacher communication: An annotated article bibliography.* Kent, OH: Kent State University Communication Research Center.

Feezel, J. D., & Rubin, R. B. (1983, February). *Assessment of pedagogical communication skills.* Paper presented at the annual meeting of the American Association of Colleges for Teacher Education, Detroit.

Harris, T. A. (1967). *I'm ok—you're ok: A practical guide to transactional analysis.* New York: Harper & Row.

Hurt, H. T., Scott, M. D., & McCroskey, J. C. (1978). *Communication in the classroom.* Reading, MA: Addison-Wesley.

Land, M. L. (1981). Combined effect of two teacher clarity variables on student achievement. *Journal of Experimental Education, 50,* 14–17.

Lynn, E. M. (1976). *Improving classroom communication: Speech communication instruction for teachers.* Annandale, VA: Speech Communication Association and ERIC Clearinghouse on Reading and Communication Skills.

41

McBath, J. H., & Jeffrey, R. C. (1978). Defining speech communication. *Communication Education, 27,* 181–188.

McCaleb, J. L. (1984). Selecting a measure of oral communication as a predictor of teaching performance. *Journal of Teacher Education, 35,* 33–38.

McCaleb, J. L., & Rosenthal, B. G. (1984). Relationships in teacher clarity between students' perceptions and observers' ratings. *Journal of Classroom Interaction, 19,* (1), 15–21.

Rosenfeld, L. B. (1983). Communication climate and coping mechanisms in the college classroom. *Communication Education, 32,* 167–174.

Rubin, R. B., & Feezel, J. D. (1985). Teacher communication competence: Essential skills and assessment procedures. *Central States Speech Journal, 36,* 4–13.

Rubin, R. B., & Feezel, J. D. (1986). Elements of teacher communication competence. *Communication Education, 35,* 254–268.

Simon, A., & Boyer, E. G. (Eds.). (1970). Mirrors for behaviors II: An anthology of observational instruments [Special Edition]. *Classroom Interaction Newsletter.*

Smith, H. A. (1979). Nonverbal communication and teaching. *Review of Educational Research, 49,* 631–672.

Speech Communication Association/American Theatre Association Joint Task Force on Teacher Preparation. (1978). *Competency models in communication and theatre for preparation and certification of elementary and secondary school specialists and non-specialists.* Washington, DC: American Theatre Association.

Staton-Spicer, A. Q., & Wulff, D. H. (1984). Research in communication and instruction: Categorization and synthesis. *Communication Education, 33,* 377–391.

Stern, D. A. (1980). Teaching and acting: A vocal analogy. *Communication Education, 29,* 259–263.

Wasserman, S. (1982). Interacting with your students, learning to hear yourself. *Childhood Education, 58,* 281–286.

Weaver, R. L., & Michel, T. A. (1983). *On lecturing: A selected bibliography.* Annandale, VA: Speech Communication Association.

3

Theory and Practice: Match or Mismatch?

Kenneth L. Brown

University of Massachusetts

W hen reading the two previous chapters, I recalled memories of a scene that took place more than 30 years ago. A young college student who sought admission to the preservice education major sat in a small room. He read aloud a selected passage to a single examiner who sat across the table from him. The examiner then asked the student some questions, made a few notations on a form, and dismissed the student. This scene was repeated many times for all students who sought admission to the "teaching major." It was the speech test. Its purpose was to verify that teacher candidates were free of articulation, voice, and fluency disorders.

We have come a long way from testing potential teachers for signs of speech problems to constructing models of teacher communication and assessing numerous communication competencies demonstrated by both preservice and inservice teachers. Today textbooks on classroom communication stress that the essence of teaching is communication; classroom communication differs from other communication situations in its purposes, environments, and participation forms; and teaching is informed by knowledge of the communication process and by practice in implementing the process (Barker, 1982; Bassett & Smythe, 1979; Cooper, 1984; Friedrich, Galvin, & Book, 1976; Hurt, Scott, & McCroskey, 1978; Klopf & Cambra, 1983; Seiler, Schuelke, & Lieb-Brilhart, 1984). Moreover, within the last decade, interdisciplinary research has focused on an interactional perspective of language use in the classroom, a perspective that examines patterns of teacher-student talk in order to understand how students learn and teachers teach through language. Underlying this research are assumptions such as the classroom is a unique communicative context, interaction in the classroom requires knowledge of pragmatic uses of language and of classroom discourse rules, and students and teachers differ in their assumptions about appropriate communicative behavior in the classroom (Green, 1983; Morine-Dershimer, 1985; Tough, 1979; Wells & Nicholls, 1985; and Wilkinson, 1982). As Cazden (1987) notes, learning to talk for academic purposes forms part of a hidden curriculum throughout the school day.

We have become increasingly precise in describing what happens in classrooms from a communicative standpoint, but we are less sure of what *should* happen. When we try to translate theory and research into practice, there is often a mismatch. As so often happens, theory and research do not answer some critical questions that practitioners face, so the practitioners forge ahead. This is the situation with oral communication. The state of the art of teaching exceeds the state of the art of assessing speaking and listening skills. States that assess teachers' speaking and listening skills are charting new ground just as are states that assess students' oral communication skills (Backlund, VanRheenen, Moore, Parks, & Booth, 1981; Rubin & Mead, 1984). Those states that implement or plan to implement measures of oral communication should be commended for recognizing the importance of oral communication in teaching and learning and addressing assessment issues in a complex domain.

The purpose of this chapter is to analyze the match between assessment practices that are described in chapter 1 and the conceptualization that Feezel describes in chapter 2. Two specific questions are addressed: (a) What perspectives on communication are stressed, and which are excluded? (b) What are some special problems of assessment in the oral communication domain?

PERSPECTIVES ON COMMUNICATION

Feezel's model of teacher communication stresses at least five key ideas: (1) Communication in the classroom is transactional. (2) Teachers need knowledge about the communication process and confidence in communicating prior to engaging in instruction. (3) Communication in the classroom is functional. (4) Some communication transactions require presentational skills, while others require interactive skills. (5) Teachers must be able to communicate effectively with different people who are involved in schooling. To what extent are these confirmed in assessment practices?

Communication is Transactional

There is a basic tension between the view typified in the model that communication is transactive and the view implemented in assessment practices that the teacher is a speaker or a listener. The transactional perspective means that teachers do not merely send information that is received intact by students. Rather, as teachers communicate with their

44

students, they simultaneously give information and, through feedback, receive information. In addition, teachers receive their own communication; they listen to themselves. Therefore, teachers and students affect each other. Both share in creating and interpreting messages. Teachers change their communication behavior in response to what they perceive another person is communicating.

Since teachers and students share in creating and interpreting messages in the transactional perspective, the traditional distinction between teacher-as-speaker and teacher-as-listener fades. This distinction stresses a linear view of communication. Yet assessment practices emphasize these distinct roles and sets of skills. Note how listening is most often assessed through standardized tests, while speaking skills are tested separately through performance measures. Interactive communication is not assessed. In fact, from an examiner's viewpoint, interaction "muddies the waters" considerably; interaction does not make for tidy testing. Yet inside and outside the classroom the bulk of speaking and listening takes place during interaction. So transactive communication seems to be an area requiring vigorous test development efforts.

One interactive teaching activity that has potential for assessment of communication skill in the classroom is the referential communication task. A speaker attempts to communicate with a listener about a target object, a referent, in a set of alternatives. The speaker's purpose might be to describe a picture or object so the listener can identify it in an array of similar pictures or objects. Or the speaker can explain how to construct a model with blocks or give a series of directions to help the listener find a destination on a map. The speaker tries to inform the listener with accuracy and efficiency, while the listener seeks to demonstrate comprehension in a goal-directed task. To be certain that the speaker and listener rely solely on verbal communication, they may not see each other; they communicate either back-to-back or across a table with a screen between them.

Teachers can engage in such tasks with students, alternating their roles as speakers and listeners. The specific tasks have been derived from a research strategy (Glucksberg, Krauss, & Higgins, 1975) but have been adapted more recently for use in the classroom (Dickson, 1981; Dickson & Patterson, 1981; McCaffrey, 1980). Since the tasks rely heavily on informative kinds of communication (describing, explaining, giving directions) and on modeling, interaction, and feedback to improve communication quality, they approximate transactive communication occurring in classroom instruction more closely than wholly separate measures.

Knowledge and Confidence

A second issue raised by the contrast between Feezel's model and assessment practices is: What learning domains are being assessed? State practices stress performance assessment. Teachers are expected to demonstrate observable behaviors such as using oral language correctly, enunciating clearly, explaining effectively, or asking higher order questions. Communication *skills* are being assessed. This is correct when the purpose is to determine whether the teacher has ability to demonstrate appropriate communicative behavior in a given situation (McCroskey, 1982).

Note that Feezel's model implies more than assessment of skills. The model is developmental because it suggests teachers need knowledge about the communication process as well as confidence in communicating prior to engaging in instructional transactions. Awareness of the communication situation is a cognitive behavior that requires relatively sophisticated analysis of who is speaking to whom, for what purpose, about what topic, and under what circumstances. The teacher is expected to understand the process of communication. This implies another form of assessment, one that measures the teacher's knowledge of communication theory. Knowledge has a bearing on performance, but performance does not always reveal one's knowledge. Each complements the other, so there is a need to assess these different domains.

Even more conspicuous is the model's emphasis on willingness to communicate and create a climate that fosters interpersonal communication. Clearly, there is a significant affective dimension to classroom communication. One part of this dimension, communication apprehension, bears directly on willingness to communicate and has been studied extensively (McCroskey, 1977). Not to be confused with fear of public speaking or "stagefright," communication apprehension is fear of real or anticipated communication encounters in both informal and formal situations. This fear is so great that the person avoids communicating whenever possible. Some research suggests that 20% of classroom teachers suffer communication apprehension, with more experiencing the problem in elementary than in secondary schools (McCroskey, 1977). Communicatively apprehensive teachers gravitate to lower grades; apparently they perceive teaching children as less threatening than teaching adolescents.

Fortunately, some measures are readily available to assess communication apprehension. The Verbal Activity Scale is one self-report measure that indicates normal verbal activity, while the Personal Report of Communication Apprehension reveals level of communication apprehension (McCroskey, 1977). Ideally, such measures would be employed early in preservice teacher preparation programs.

Assessment needs to recognize that a teacher's success depends on communication performance in the classroom. Underlying performance should be a knowledge base that can support communicating in more situations than can be observed in a single assessment and an attitude that reflects willingness to communicate and confidence in communicating.

46

A Range of Communication Situations

In the third, fourth, and fifth points summarized earlier, Feezel's model emphasizes that teachers communicate in a range of situations. These situations occur in moments of instructional transaction as well as in extra-class exchanges and are defined by different functions, forms (or what Feezel calls "modes"), and audiences.

The five communication functions that Feezel cites are derived from research on communication development (Wells, 1973) and have been applied in classroom activities (Allen, Brown, & Yatvin, 1986; Wood, 1977a, 1977b). The functions imply that the teacher must possess and be able to draw from a repertoire of communication acts. Convincing parents, persuading a school administrator, praising and encouraging students, explaining information, facilitating social interaction, role-playing a problem in class, speculating about a solution, and other similar acts are required daily. But by emphasizing explaining and questioning acts, assessment practices stress one function, informing. An exception is the few states that assess giving directions, which stresses the controlling function. Evaluators, then, need to consider how important other communication functions are and how those functions can be assessed.

Multiple forms of communication also need to be assessed. Teachers must be able to conduct one-on-one conferences and interviews, lecture to a class, read materials aloud, lead class discussions, organize small-group tasks, ask questions, and respond to answers. Feezel notes that some of these forms require presentational skills and others interactive skills. But presentational forms dominate in assessment practices. Of the 12 competency categories that are assessed, 3 stress the interactive skills of feedback, questioning, and using student ideas. Seven categories point to an emphasis on presentational speaking: oral language usage, speech mechanics, fluency, explaining, directing, emphasis and enthusiasm, and nonverbal cues.

Research in presentational speaking (Becker, 1962; Price, 1964) has exhibited relative consistency in evaluation criteria. Although speech rating scales might contain at least 11 items, raters make only a limited number of judgments that cluster around a few general aspects of presentation such as language, delivery, content, and organization. Language and delivery skills (mechanics, fluency, enthusiasm) appear to be stressed more in assessment practices than matters of content and organization such as making key ideas clear, supporting ideas with appropriate examples and data, adhering to the topic, and conveying ideas in an understandable order.

Communication with students is spotlighted in assessment practices although teachers need to be able to communicate with other audiences such as parents, peers, administrators, and professional leaders. The classroom is the primary assessment arena. Thus assessment practices sample only part of the range of communication situations the teacher faces. A particular view of teacher communication that emerges is: The teacher's primary function is to disseminate information through presentational speaking to a student audience. States that plan to assess teacher-parent communication bear watching, though, for they may discover ways to assess communication in larger school and community contexts.

For Further Consideration

As teacher education programs and state agencies continue to explore ways to assess oral communication, further consideration needs to be given to the level of communication skills that is the focus of assessment, ways teachers use language in teaching, and importance of role taking and audience analysis.

First, a distinction must be made in the levels of skills that are the focus of assessment. Competencies are stated in behavioral terms and assessed as skills through performance measures. Following analyses of Polanyi (1964), Scheffler (1965), and Cazden (1972), instruction and assessment can focus on two skill levels: facilities and critical skills. Facilities are subsidiary in awareness to critical skills, which demand our focal attention. Thus facilities are components of and serve higher order critical skills. From the list discussed in chapter 1, facilities include speaking clearly at an appropriate pace and volume, using grammar correctly, using correct vowel/consonant/diphthong sounds, varying vocal intensity and rate, and speaking fluently. Critical skills include explaining, questioning, and giving directions.

Evaluators have to decide at what level to focus assessment. Should the focus be on particular facilities, as it appears to be in some schemes, or should it be on critical skills? By focusing on functional tasks—giving directions, persuading, narrating, describing, explaining—several facilities can be assessed and strengthened simultaneously, not as ends in themselves, but as behaviors that are instrumental in accomplishing a larger instructional goal.

Second, teacher educators and evaluators must consider the role of language in teaching. Assessment practices appear to stress one aspect of language, correct usage. But there are other ways to observe the role of language in education. Teachers need to recognize and use language as an instrument for learning. This implies reducing the gulf between students' language and the language of textbooks (Olson, 1981) and teachers (Barnes, Britton, & Rosen, 1969). According to Barnes et al. (1969), this gulf stems, at least in part, from specialist language and the language of education. Specialist language refers to vocabulary that is inherent in learning a subject. To learn mathematics students must master concepts

48

such as "parallel" and "multiples"; in music, terms such as "pitch," "treble clef," and "embouchure" must be mastered; and in English, students must learn "homonyms," "stanza," "meter," and "onomatopoeia." For the student, learning a subject involves comprehending and using the subject's vocabulary.

The language of education refers to expository language used by the teacher but not specific to any school subject. For example, the teacher says, "The point I want to make is . . ." or "It is still quite apparent today that. . . ." Here language serves a sociocultural function by identifying the speaker's role as teacher and relationship to listener as voice of authority. At other times the teacher says, "*The position of* line A *in relation to* line B . . ." or asks, "What two things do these examples have *in common?*" This language serves a conceptual function; the italicized phrases carry essential thought processes of the lesson.

Teachers use language to support their instructional role and to perform conceptual functions. Both purposes occur together for the teacher, but for students the teacher's language first has a sociocultural function. Students understand the teacher's talk as "the kind of thing my teacher says." For students, language serves the conceptual function only after they can use the language in their thinking, talking, and writing. To learn through language, students must do their own telling, asking, classifying, ordering, explaining, narrating, and recording.

From an assessment standpoint, evaluators can look beyond the teacher's grammar to specialist uses of language and the language of education. Are teachers aware of these uses? Do teachers take steps to help students understand these uses? A "yes" to both questions would help solve many of the communication problems that occur in classrooms.

Third, assessment should consider role taking, a process that is instrumental to effective and appropriate communication. Not to be confused with role playing, which involves overtly enacting the attributes of another person, role taking is a covert, cognitive process. Role taking involves apprehending and understanding critical attributes of our listeners or audience. These attributes include the listener's knowledge and experience with the subject; factors that might influence the listener to understand or not understand our message and agree or disagree; the listener's mood, age, and sex; and the listener's motivations, attitudes, and beliefs.

Flavell, Botkins, Fry Jr., Wright, and Jarvis (1975) have identified five cognitive requisites to role taking. Speakers need to know: other people's perceptions, thoughts, and feelings differ from their own; it is useful to analyze the other person's attributes in order to realize their own goal; how to analyze accurately and predict the most important attributes; how to remember these attributes, considering one's goal and viewpoint; and how to translate into an effective message what they know about the other person's attributes.

49

I am not suggesting that role taking should be the object of assessment. Role taking serves and is manifested in audience analysis, which in turn results in adapted communication. Yet, this process does not appear to be prominent in assessment practices. Perhaps some evidence exists in pedagogical content knowledge, the ability to organize and interpret content so students can understand. But the process deserves to be more prominent because it is essential for knowing how to gain and maintain students' attention, connecting new ideas with students' previous knowledge and experience, elaborating and clarifying major ideas, relating materials to students' cultural and ethnic backgrounds, and choosing language that is readily understood. To teach effectively, teachers must engage in role taking and adapt to their students' perspectives.

ASSESSMENT ISSUES IN ORAL COMMUNICATION

The assessment process merits attention in oral communication. In the past five years there have been at least five reviews of oral communication assessment instruments (Backlund, VanRheenan, Moore, Parks, & Booth, 1981; Brown, Backlund, Gurry, & Jandt, 1979; Larson, Backlund, Redmond, & Barbour, 1978; Rubin & Mead, 1984; Rubin, Sisco, Moore, & Quianthy, 1983). While many of these instruments are for use with students, their development informs teacher assessment. There is no dearth of measures for assessing different aspects of oral communication, and there is no aspect of functional communication for which measurement problems are prohibitive (Larson, 1978). But there are problems. Rubin and Mead (1984) identify 28 research and development priorities. Space limitations prohibit discussion of all these priorities, but a few pertaining to teacher assessment need to be presented briefly.

Validity

First, there appears to be little consensus on a conception of oral communication competence that guides assessment. In chapter 1 McCaleb exposes some communication competencies that are incorporated within other domains such as subject knowledge, diversity of instructional method, and classroom management. Where, for example, does classroom management end and effective communication begin? Larson (1978) suggests that the lack of conceptual clarity is the greatest long-run impediment facing communication assessment. Second, we need comprehensive surveys of objectives in courses on instructional or classroom communication. Third, if we have a common conception and common objectives there is still a need to decide how to best sample the oral communication domain. Situations that are commonly taught in some classes such as giving a speech, reading aloud, or participating in and leading a discussion,

50

are not equivalent. Fourth, clear evaluation criteria need to be established. Assessment practices vary in the way they define and weight criteria such as oral language, speech mechanics, or content and organization. Fifth, given adequate sampling and clear evaluation criteria, there is a need to establish how well performance in assessment situations coincides with performance in daily classroom instruction.

Reliability

Three reliability issues are evident. First, it is unclear whether teachers are evaluated by different observers and, if so, whether there is a high degree of agreement among observers. Training aimed at calibrating observers needs to be an integral part of assessment programs. A second issue is equivalence of topics and tasks. Some assessment situations vary the discourse topic and task without establishing equivalence. For example, how is a teacher's performance in explaining how to make an object related to performance in asking questions or in telling a personal narrative? Third, to what extent is "test-retest" reliability sought? How many times is a teacher observed in order to determine oral communication proficiency? How many samples of communication are used?

Bias

Stiggins (1981) notes that care must be taken to deal with potential sources of bias in assessment because patterns of oral communication are greatly affected by divergent linguistic and cultural factors. One possible bias source is the assessment situation. Is it familiar and comfortable for the teacher and students? The physical surroundings and the race, sex, and manner of the evaluator, particularly in a face-to-face oral communication situation, can affect the behaviors of the teachers and students who are being observed. Also, bias can arise when evaluators' judgments are influenced more by their social attitudes and experiences than by clear rating criteria and standards, particularly in assessment of speaking performance. Stiggins (1981) emphasizes that performance tests must be developed by persons knowledgeable about and sensitive to the cultural and social experiences and traditions of the persons to be tested.

Feasibility

Beyond issues of validity, reliability, and bias is the matter of cost. Cost translates into feasibility. Even when state assessment projects recognize the importance of oral communication skills and want to pursue assessment, they may lack the necessary resources. Many speech performance measures require individual administrations. Listening assessment requires tape recorded instructions and response options. Compared with presumably more efficient group administered written tests, oral communication measures can seem less feasible. So there is a need to develop cost-benefit analyses—cost in terms of time, money, and equipment, and benefit in terms of the assessment's effect on teacher performance and classroom practice.

In summary, the assessment of teachers' basic communication skills is a complex process that must consider the transactive nature of communication, evidence of the teacher's underlying knowledge and affective behaviors as well as performance skills, the teacher's ability to communicate functionally in a range of situations, the level of skill to be assessed, the role of language in learning, and the importance of adapted communication. In addition, assessment in the oral communication domain must address validity, reliability, bias, and feasibility issues.

Let us not forget that assessment is a communication process. Assessment can be used to certify proficiency among individual teachers. But more important, assessment should be used as a constructive tool that informs teachers, improves their communication behavior, and results in positive effects on classroom practices.

References

Allen, R. R., Brown, K. L., & Yatvin, J. (1986). *Learning language through communication: A functional perspective.* Belmont, CA: Wadsworth.

Backlund, P., VanRheenan, D., Moore, M., Parks, A. M., & Booth, J. (1981). A national survey of state practices in speaking and listening assessment. In Clearinghouse for Applied Performance Testing, *Perspectives on the assessment of speaking and listening skills for the 1980s* (pp. 3–24). Portland, OR: Northwest Regional Educational Laboratory.

Barker, L. L. (Ed.). (1982). *Communication in the classroom: Original essays.* Englewood Cliffs, NJ: Prentice-Hall.

Barnes, D., Britton, J., & Rosen, J. (1969). *Language, the learner and the school.* Harmondsworth, Middlesex, England: Penguin.

Bassett, R. E., & Smythe, M. (1979). *Communication and instruction.* New York: Harper and Row.

Becker, S. L. (1962). The rating of speeches: Scale independence. *Speech Monographs, 29,* 38–44.

Brown, K. L., Backlund, P., Gurry, J., & Jandt, F. (1979). *Assessment of basic speaking and listening skills.* Boston: Massachusetts Department of Education. (ERIC Document Reproduction Service No. ED 178 969)

Cazden, C. B. (1972). *Child language and education.* New York: Holt, Rinehart & Winston.

Cazden, C. B. (1987). English for academic purposes: The student-talk register. *English Education, 19,* 31–43.

Cooper, P. J. (1984). *Speech communication for the classroom teacher.* Dubuque, IA: Gorsuch-Scarisbrick.

Dickson, W. P. (1981). Referential communication activities in research and in the curriculum: A metaanalysis. In W. P. Dickson (Ed.), *Children's oral communication skills* (pp. 189–204). New York: Academic Press.

Dickson, W. P., & Patterson, J. H. (1981). Evaluating referential communication games for teaching speaking and listening skills. *Communication Education, 30,* 11–22.

Flavell, J. H., Botkin, P., Fry, C. L., Jr., Wright, J. W., & Jarvis, P. E. (1975). *The development of role-taking and communication skills in children.* Huntington, NY: Robert E. Krieger.

Friedrich, G. W., Galvin, K. M., & Book, C. L. (1976). *Growing together . . . classroom communication.* Columbus, OH: Charles E. Merrill.

Green, J. L. (1983). Research on teaching as a linguistic process: A state of the art. In E. W. Gordon (Ed.), *Review of research in education, 10* (pp. 151–252). Washington, DC: American Educational Research Association.

Glucksberg, S., Krauss, R., & Higgins, E. T. (1975). The development of referential communication skills. In F. D. Horowitz (Ed.), *Review of child development research* (Vol. 4) (pp. 305–345). Chicago: University of Chicago Press.

Hurt, H. T., Scott, M. D., & McCroskey, J. C. (1978). *Communication in the classroom.* Reading, MA: Addison-Wesley.

Klopf, D. W., & Cambra, R. E. (1983). *Speaking skills for prospective teachers.* Englewood, CO: Morton.

Larson, C. E. (1978). Problems in assessing functional communication. *Communication Education, 27,* 304–309.

Larson, C., Backlund, P., Redmond, M., & Barbour, A. (1978). *Assessing functional communication.* Annandale, VA: Speech Communication Association/ERIC Clearinghouse on Reading and Communication Skills.

McCaffrey, A. (1980). *Testing a model of communicative competence in the classroom. Final report.* (NIE Project No. G-76-0042). Washington, DC: National Institute of Education.

McCroskey, J. C. (1977). *Quiet children and the classroom teacher.* Annandale, VA: Speech Communication Association/ERIC Clearinghouse on Reading and Communication Skills.

McCroskey, J. C. (1982). Communication competence and performance: A research and pedagogical perspective. *Communication Education, 31,* 1–7.

Morine-Dershimer, G. (1985). *Talking, listening and learning in elementary classrooms.* New York: Longman.

Olson, D. R. (1981). Writing: The divorce of the author from the text. In B. M. Kroll and R. J. Vann (Eds.), *Exploring speaking-writing relations: Connections and contrasts* (pp. 99–110). Urbana, IL: National Council of Teachers of English.

Polanyi, M. (1964). *Personal knowledge: Towards a post-critical philosophy.* New York: Harper and Row.

Price, W. K. (1964). *The University of Wisconsin speech attainment test.* Unpublished dissertation, University of Wisconsin.

Rubin, D. L., & Mead, N. A. (1984). *Large scale assessment of oral communication skills: Kindergarten through grade 12.* Annandale, VA: Speech Communication Association/ERIC Clearinghouse on Reading and Communication Skills.

Rubin, R. B., Sisco, J., Moore, M. R., & Quianthy, R. (1983). *Oral communication assessment procedures and instrument development in higher education.* Annandale, VA: Speech Communication Association.

Scheffler, I. (1965). *Conditions of knowledge.* Chicago: Scott, Foresman.

Seiler, W. J., Schuelke, L. D., & Lieb-Brilhart, B. (1984). *Communication for the contemporary classroom.* New York: Holt, Rinehart and Winston.

Stiggins, R. J. (1981). Potential sources of bias in speaking and listening assessment. In Clearinghouse for Applied Performance Testing, *Perspectives on the assessment of speaking and listening skills for the 1980s* (pp. 43–49). Portland, OR: Northwest Regional Educational Laboratory.

Tough, J. (1979). *Talk for teaching and learning.* Portsmouth, NH: Heinemann.

Wells, G. (1973). *Coding manual for the description of child speech.* Bristol, England: School of Education, University of Bristol.

Wells, G., & Nicholls, J. (Eds.) (1985). *Language and learning: An interactional perspective.* Philadelphia: Falmer Press.

Wilkinson, L. C. (1982). *Communicating in the classroom.* New York: Academic Press.

Wood, B. S. (Ed.) (1977a). *Development of functional communication competencies: Grades 7–12.* Annandale, VA: Speech Communication Association/ERIC Clearinghouse on Reading and Communication Skills.

Wood, B. S. (Ed.) (1977b). *Development of functional communication competencies: Pre-K–grade 6.* Annandale, VA: Speech Communication Association/ERIC Clearinghouse on Reading and Communication Skills.

4

A Critique of the
Research Base for Assessing
Communication Skills
of Teachers

Cassandra L. Book and Gerald G. Duffy*

Michigan State University

T he research base for evaluating teachers' communication skills comes from two areas. Process-product research (attempts to link teacher behavior to student achievement) and associated principles of direct instruction (e.g., teacher explicit instruction of concepts and principles to be learned) comprise one area. The second is speech communication research. The criteria often are stated in behavioral terms so they can be easily observed and quantified. While the findings of process-product, direct instruction, and speech communication research are important and should be considered when evaluating teachers' communication skills, they have limitations for teacher assessment. Furthermore, some of the most recent research on effective instruction suggests that additional communication skills, more subtle and fluid than those emphasized on current assessment instruments, are much more important than what is included on behavioral checklists. This chapter summarizes the results of early research and their limitations for teacher assessment, contrasts those findings with recent research, which suggests more subtle communication skills play a crucial role in effective teaching, and raises cautions about the assessment of teachers' communication skills.

A CRITIQUE OF THE RESEARCH BASE OF
CURRENT ASSESSMENT EFFORTS

T he research base of current assessment efforts can be divided into two sections: results from research on teaching and results from

*Coauthors listed in alphabetical order.

speech communication studies. We have concerns regarding how both are applied to teacher evaluation.

Critique of Research on Teaching Findings

Knowledge about pedagogy has increased in the last 15 years. Much of this research has been summarized by Brophy and Good (1986). Although it is unnecessary to repeat what these authors have so thoroughly documented, we will briefly highlight some of the major findings and our concerns about the use of these findings in teacher evaluation instruments.

Our first concern is that behavioral checklists do not accurately reflect the complex data obtained from research on teaching. For example, teacher questioning has received much attention with Brophy and Good (1986) discussing: 1) difficulty level of questions; 2) cognitive level of questions; 3) clarity of questions; 4) post-question wait time; 5) selecting the respondent; 6) waiting for the student to respond; 7) reactions to correct responses; 8) reacting to partly correct responses; 9) reacting to incorrect responses; and 10) reacting to students' questions and comments. By translating such a complex set of findings into discrete items about questioning on a checklist, there is the danger that the complexity and interactions will be masked and false conclusions about teachers' effectiveness will result.

Second, we are concerned that research on teaching findings is being used in teacher assessment instruments without appropriate regard for context. For example, Evertson, Anderson, Anderson, and Brophy (1980), Evertson, Anderson, and Brophy (1978), and Evertson, Emmer, and Brophy (1980) examined how findings apply differently at various grade levels. In summarizing this research, Brophy and Good (1986) state, "Most findings must be qualified by grade level, type of objective, type of student, and other context factors" (p. 366). Thus, the evaluative criteria, while grounded in teacher behaviors that research says make a difference in student learning, are sometimes inappropriately applied to various grade levels or contexts. This seems to be a serious limitation in current assessment instruments.

Third, we are concerned that findings are applied to teacher assessment instruments without regard for the curricular outcome. For example, the value of structuring lessons and actively involving students through the use of questions was documented in a series of studies done at the University of Canterbury in New Zealand (Hughes, 1973; Nuthall & Church, 1973; Wright & Nuthall, 1970). Similarly, Stallings et al. (1974, 1977, 1978) found achievement gains to be positively associated with active group instruction in the subject matter; and Anderson, Evertson, and Brophy (1979) developed principles for organizing, managing, and instructing group reading sessions. All these findings, however, focused on basic skills achievement as measured by achievement tests. They may be less appropriate when the curricular outcomes are conceptual or aesthetic understandings. Current teacher assessment instruments, however, do not make such curricular distinctions.

Critique of Speech Communication Research

We have similar concerns regarding speech communication research. Of the several communication categories identified by McCaleb in chapter 1, oral language usage and speech mechanics can be combined. Those factors, while important, are insufficient for learning to occur. Students must be able to hear and understand a teacher to learn, but hearing and understanding a teacher do not assure that learning will occur. Regarding correct language usage, one may argue that the teacher is a powerful role model for students and that improper language usage may teach students poor grammar or poor expression. Such language usage, however, does not necessarily interfere with the students' ability to learn the content. Improper language use may influence the teachers' credibility with high school students and thus interfere with the teachers' effectiveness but, again, these qualities are not necessarily linked to student learning.

We also are concerned with the category of "enthusiasm" or references to the teacher communicating subject matter information with confidence and authority. The topic of ethos or source credibility has been discussed by communication researchers and scholars since the days of Aristotle and has been recently defined, in part, as dynamism (McCroskey, 1968). Such enthusiasm or dynamism may build a teacher's credibility or the students' perception of the teacher's effectiveness. Studies by Norton (1983) link characteristics of a dynamic teaching style, which may include an enthusiastic delivery, with students' perceptions of teachers' effectiveness. As Brophy and Good (1986) state, "Enthusiasm, usually measured by high inference ratings, appears to be more related to affective than to cognitive outcomes" (p. 362). Thus, teacher assessment instruments that include the criteria of teacher enthusiasm may be contributing to positive affect, but not necessarily to increased achievement. We concur with the Georgia assessment that cautions enthusiasm alone is insufficient for effective instruction.

Summary of Critique of Research Base

The effective teaching research has emphasized overt teacher behaviors and task engagement. For instance, Brophy and Good (1986) reported that many teacher effectiveness findings focus on control of pupil behavior and learning tasks. Effective teachers select certain tasks for students to pursue and ensure that students concentrate on these tasks during instruction. Hence, quantity and pacing of instruction gets emphasized, and the teacher's role as an active supervisor of students' task completion efforts is stressed. Instruction is conceptualized in terms of the lesson, with instructional functions limited to sequential lesson events such as review, presentation, guided practice, feedback, and independent practice (Good & Grouws, 1979; Rosenshine & Stevens, 1984). Within the lesson, emphasis is on being explicit, clear, specific, and structured, and a heavy emphasis is on questioning in a recitation mode (Brophy & Good, 1986; Rosenshine & Stevens, 1984). Such findings cannot be applied to teacher evaluation as if these factors do not interact and there are no context effects nor can they be applied equally to all curricular outcomes. Similarly, the speech communication research has emphasized overt traits such as speech patterns and enthusiasm. These, too, are important, but they are insufficient for evaluating teacher performance.

NEW DIRECTIONS REFLECTED IN
RECENT INSTRUCTIONAL RESEARCH

There is no question about the importance of student engagement on task and structuring the lesson appropriately, necessity for being specific and explicit during the lesson, or desirability for proper language usage and enthusiasm. When evaluating teachers' communication skills, these criteria must be included. Some recent research, however, suggests that these necessary criteria are insufficient to achieve the most effective instruction. A series of studies on teacher effectiveness during reading instruction (Duffy, Roehler, & Wesselman, 1985) serve as an example.

Two conflicting sets of research findings triggered the reading instruction studies. First, recent research on reading emphasizes the need for readers to be strategic, that is, systematic and deliberate in applying skills in decoding and making sense of the text. Second, studies of practices employed by teachers indicated that the teaching of mental acts associated with strategic reading were seldom emphasized during classroom instruction (Duffy & McIntyre, 1982; Durkin, 1978–79). Instead, classroom practice studies revealed an emphasis on student engagement on task and structured lesson sequences such as those found in the effectiveness teaching research. There was a heavy emphasis on step-by-step questioning procedures, which focus students on task completion rather than mental acts involved in being strategic. As a result, students were left to infer these mental processes.

Consequently, the studies were initiated to determine whether student awareness of how to use skills and ability to read would increase if teachers were explicit in explaining the reason involved in using reading skills as strategies. For example, assume a teacher was teaching the reading skill "compound words." The teacher's guide recommended directing students to complete a worksheet by drawing lines between the two words in the compound and to say the word. To explain the strategic reasoning, the teacher would 1) identify a forthcoming reading situation in which students will find an unknown compound word; 2) teach students to stop reading when they recognize the word is unknown; 3) show them how to search their repertoire of strategies for one that can be used to identify the unknown word; and 4) make statements about how to seek recognizable word parts, combine mentally the meaning of the two words, and think about the combined meaning to determine whether it makes sense in the text.

Two descriptive and two experimental studies were conducted over a four-year period. The results indicate that when teachers explicitly explain mental acts associated with using skills as strategies students are more aware and achieve better than when only task engagement and lesson structure are emphasized (Roehler, Duffy, Putnam, Wesselman, Sivan, Rackliffe, Book, Meloth, & Vavrus, 1986; Duffy, Roehler, & Wesselman, 1985). In addition, *post hoc* qualitative analysis of the most effective teachers suggests that evaluations of teacher communication skills need to go beyond the task involvement and lesson structure elements currently emphasized (Duffy, Roehler, & Rackliffe, 1986). Three examples, which reflect a more subtle and fluid concept of instructional communication than what is traditionally found in the teacher effectiveness research, follow.

Modeling and Responsive Interactions

Virtually all literature on effective teaching emphasizes the need to demonstrate for students and interact with them. Most of the emphasis, however, is on giving directions to complete tasks and feedback regarding the correctness or incorrectness of student responses.

It is important for teachers to know that students understand how to follow directions and that they receive feedback on the correctness of their responses. The most effective teachers go beyond these behaviors during instruction. They focus on making visible the *thinking* involved in completing the task rather than just the overt steps to be followed. They listen to students' responses to decide what additional modeling of the mental processing is required as well as to provide feedback about correctness and incorrectness.

Consequently, the more effective teachers focus on communicating information about the thinking processes involved rather than only the steps required to complete the worksheet or skill page. This communication requires a spontaneity and responsiveness that goes beyond the presentation of prepared models and demonstrations. Teachers model and then ask students to perform the same task in order to determine

60

whether the students employ appropriate reasoning. The teacher observes the students' reasoning. If the responses indicate misunderstandings, the teacher goes beyond corrective feedback by providing reexplanations and elaborations designed to bring students closer to the desired understanding. This interactive cycle is the heart of instruction where the teacher mediates the students' responses to decide what needs to be explained next and students mediate the teacher's elaborations to decide how to modify their understandings.

During this series of interactions, which occur over time, students are moved from what Vygotskey (1978) calls "other-directed to self-directed" in their understanding and use of what is being taught. How quickly or how slowly the teacher moves the student toward the "self-directed" mode and what the teacher says and does to expedite this movement are fluid and tentative endeavors.

The communication required here is more sophisticated than what is normally discussed in the traditional teacher effectiveness research. It requires a spontaneity, sensitivity to students' mental processes, and a fluidity that is much more characteristic of conversation than of traditional lessons. This essence of instructional communication should be assessed but rarely is. It illustrates the concept of communication as a "transactional, symbolic process" (Miller, 1980). The transactional approach is consistent with the perspective of communication as the process of sharing meaning.

Achieving Conceptual Consistency

Ways in which the most effective teachers achieve a conceptual consistency in their teaching provide a second illustration of how effective instructional communication is more subtle than previously thought. The most effective teachers are explicit and structured during lessons, and they are explicit and structured about the same thing in every lesson. They communicate to students a consistent message. Instruction acquires a cohesive element in an individual lesson and in many lessons taught across the academic year.

One example of this instructional characteristic is the way in which effective teachers communicate the usefulness of instructional content. In the study of teaching skills as strategies cited above, effective teachers informed students when the skill being taught would be used, the problem the skill would solve, and why the skill should be learned. More important, they gave the same message during every lesson. Whether the skill being taught was phonics or main idea, the effective teachers typically began lessons by showing students examples of when they could use that skill. Thus, the teachers consistently reinforced the concept that skills were to be used to solve problems encountered in reading.

61

Such conceptual consistency brings a glue to instruction and combats the tendency to teach lesson content in isolated chunks. When conceptual understandings are consistently presented and applied in similar ways, the instruction assumes a level of meaningfulness that enhances effectiveness. This important aspect of instructional communication is found infrequently in teacher assessment instruments.

The Longitudinal Aspect of Instruction

A third subtle aspect of instruction is that teaching takes time. Seldom is the instructional issue settled in a single lesson.

In the studies used for illustration, a major outcome measure was student interviews following lessons. During these interviews, students were asked to tell what skill was being taught and when and how to use the skill. Lessons were observed at intervals year-round, and teachers' explanations and students' responses to interviews were monitored. Teachers who had been taught how to improve their instructional explanations about using reading skills showed immediate and statistically significant improvement in these explanations during the Fall of the academic year. Their students, however, showed no significant growth in lesson content awareness until February because they construct meaning gradually. As Doyle (1983) and Winne and Marx (1982) note, students "mediate" instructional information, using their unique background knowledge to construct understandings about what they are supposed to learn. Thus, students do not learn immediately what the teacher intends. Instead, they gradually restructure instructional information and build appropriate understandings over time. Learning seldom occurs in a single lesson, but most teacher assessment instruments are designed to be used in single, isolated observations.

Summary of New Research Directions

The overt and behavioral characteristics of effective teaching such as those associated with student engagement on task, lesson structure, language usage, and enthusiasm are important to note when examining teachers' communication skills. More recent research, however, suggests that instruction is a more subtle and fluid endeavor than implied in the earlier teaching and speech communication findings. Those findings may lead to necessary but insufficient criteria for effective instructional communication. This recent research suggests that instructional communication requires a sensitivity to student *understandings* as well as to their answers. There should be an ability to respond to misunderstandings with spontaneous elaborations and clarifications. Instructional communication requires a conceptual linking of the individual lessons so a consistency and cohesion is brought to instruction. It requires time because student learning is a process of gradually constructing knowledge. These findings put teachers' communication skills in a new light and have implications for the focus of assessment efforts.

CONCLUSION

Any assessment instrument has an ideal image, or concept, of the person or thing being measured. Statewide assessments of teachers' communication competencies also have images or concepts of an effective teacher. We recognize that the definition of an effective teacher may be based on several factors including such items as: 1) a perception held by students, principals, parents, or colleagues of teachers' effectiveness; 2) the teacher's ability to enhance the positive self-concept of learners and their affective development; 3) the ability to build a social climate in the classroom to enhance the learning of students in groups; 4) the ability to promote appreciation for diversity within a student population; 5) the ability to effectively manage the classroom to avoid disruptions. We also recognize that teachers can be taught to engage in effective communication behaviors resulting in positive student achievement (Roehler, et. al. 1986). Teacher assessment instruments have potential value for strengthening teacher communication behavior because they focus on effective teaching behaviors and provide guidelines for improving teaching. The extent to which such assessment instruments can enhance teachers' and administrators' awareness of a pedagogical knowledge base is beneficial.

Cautions are required, however. Brophy and Good (1986) list significant reasons for not translating research findings on teacher behavior and student achievement into a teacher assessment instrument, stating "there may be different but functionally equivalent paths to the same outcome" (p. 366). Effective teaching behaviors may not be structured or ordered in the exact way that emerged from the research. Brophy and Good (1986) also emphasize that their teacher behavior research review provides evidence of academic achievement only. Thus the findings do not include other teacher objectives such as "fostering positive attitudes, personal development, and good group relations" (p. 366). These authors note that teachers have multiple goals when teaching rather than just achievement; data from many of the process-product studies come from traditionally taught classrooms; and "most findings must be qualified by grade level, type of objective, type of student, and other context factors" (p. 366). Thus, states that have developed assessment instruments based on process-product research need to be cautioned about applying those findings to a heterogeneous mix of students being taught multiple objectives in the context of the sometimes competing demands of the classroom.

We also are concerned about the use of assessment instruments that are theoretically defensible because they are based on research findings.

First, open-ended instruments are highly dependent on observers' perceptions, understanding of effective communication, and attentiveness to communication detail in the classroom. Observers can be trained, but the weakness of relying solely on observer perceptions creates potential disadvantages for teachers. Second, behavior checklists are limited. They assume a one-to-one correspondence between teacher behavior and student achievement that may not exist. The teaching-learning process is a more complex, dynamic, interactive process than the behavior checklist suggests. As Hermann (1986) notes, there is a danger that the qualitative dimensions of instruction will be ignored. Third, a question is raised regarding how much of a certain behavior must be lacking in order to make a teacher ineffective. The assessment instruments that provide uniform weighting of criteria may negate the importance of the accuracy of information being presented.

We urge educators to continue participating in the development of the pedagogical knowledge base by (1) systematically reviewing the effect of their communication behaviors in the classroom and documenting changes that they make in affecting student learning and by (2) supporting researchers who wish to do naturalistic studies in their classrooms. Only through systematic and sustained effort to understand the phenomena of effective instruction and the effects of teacher behavior on student achievement will we be able to more systematically prepare teachers to be professional educators. Meanwhile, we must guard against a misuse of the research base and the simplistic diluting of findings to fit an assessment purpose.

References

Anderson, L., Evertsen, C., & Brophy, J. (1979). An experimental study of effective teaching in first-grade reading groups. *Elementary School Journal, 79*, 193–223.

Brophy, J., & Good, T. (1986). Teacher behavior and student achievement. In M. Wittrock (Ed.). *The handbook of research on teaching,* (3rd ed.) (pp. 328–375). New York: MacMillan.

Doyle, W. (1983). Academic work. *Review of Educational Research, 53,* (2), 159–199.

Duffy, G., & McIntyre, L. (1982). A naturalistic study of instructional assistance in primary grade reading. *Elementary School Journal, 83*(1), 15–23.

Duffy, G., Roehler, L., & Rackliffe, G. (1986). How teachers' instructional talk influences students' understanding of lesson content. *Elementary School Journal, 87*(1), 3–16.

Duffy, G., Roehler, L, & Wesselman, R. (1985). Disentangling the complexities of instructional effectiveness: A line of research on classroom reading instruction. In J. Niles & R. Lelik (Eds.), *Issues in literacy: A research perspective* (pp. 244–250). Rochester, NY: National Reading Conference.

Durkin, D. (1978–79). What classroom observations reveal about reading comprehension instruction. *Reading Research Quarterly, 14,* 481–533.

Evertson, C., Anderson, C., Anderson, L., & Brophy, J. (1980). Relationships between classroom behaviors and student outcomes in junior high mathematics and English classes. *American Educational Research Journal, 17,* 43–60.

Evertson, C., Anderson, L., & Brophy, J. (1978). *Texas Junior High School Study: Final report of process-outcome relationships* (Report No. 4061). Austin: University of Texas, R & D Center for Teacher Education.

Evertson, C., Emmer, E., & Brophy, J. (1980). Predictors of effective teaching in junior high mathematics classrooms. *Journal for Research in Mathematics Education, 11,* 167–178.

Good, T. L., & Grouws, D. A. (1979). The Missouri mathematics effectiveness project. *Journal of Educational Psychology, 71,* 143–155.

Herrmann, B. A. (1986). *Effective teacher evaluation: A quantitative and qualitative process.* Unpublished manuscript, University of South Carolina, Columbia.

Hughes, D. (1973). An experimental investigation of the effects of pupil responding and teacher reaction on pupil achievement. *American Educational Journal, 10,* 21–37.

McCroskey, J. C. (1968). *An introduction to rhetorical communication.* Englewood Cliffs, NJ: Prentice-Hall.

Miller, G. R. (1980). Introduction to communication. In C. L. Book (Ed.) *Human communication: Principles, contexts, and skills* (pp. 4–38). New York: St. Martin's Press.

Norton, R. (1983). *Communicator style: Theory, applications, and measures.* Beverly Hills: Sage Publications.

Nuthall, G., & Church, J. (1973). Experimental studies of teaching behaviour. In G. Chanan (Ed.)., *Towards a science of teaching.* London: National Foundation for Educational Research.

Roehler, L., Duffy, G., Putnam, J., Wesselman, R., Sivan, E., Rackliffe, G., Book, C., Meloth, M., & Vavrus, L. (1986). *The effect of direct explanation of reading strategies on third graders' awareness and achievement: A technical report of the 1984–85 study.* (Research Series No. 181). East Lansing: Michigan State University, Institute for Research on Teaching.

Rosenshine, B., & Stevens, R. (1984). Instructional functions. In P. D. Pearson (Ed.), *Handbook of reading research* (pp. 745–798). New York: Longman.

Stallings, J., & Kaskowitz, D. (1974). *Follow through. Classroom observation evaluation 1972–1973* (SRI Project URU-7370). Stanford, CA: Stanford Research Institute.

Stallings, J., Cory, R., Fairweather, J., & Needels, M. (1977). *Early Childhood Education Classroom Evaluation.* Menlo Park, CA: SRI International.

Stallings, J., Cory, R., Fairweather, J., & Needels, M. (1978). *A study of basic reading skills taught in secondary schools.* Menlo Park, CA: SRI International.

Vygotskey, L. (1978). *Mind and society.* (M. Cole, V. John-Steiner, S. Scrubner, & E. Sonberman, Trans.), Cambridge, MA: Harvard University Press.

Winne, P., & Marx, R. (1982). Students' and teachers' views of thinking processes for classroom learning. *Elementary School Journal, 82,* 493–518.

Wright, C., & Nuthall, G. (1970). Relationships between teacher behaviors and pupil achievement in three experimental elementary science lessons. *American Educational Research Journal, 7,* 477–491.

5

Is Assessing Communication An Exercise in Miscommunication?

Renee T. Clift

University of Houston

Several years ago many speech department offices were decorated with a poster reading, "I know that you think that you heard what I said, but I am not certain that what you heard is what I really meant." This protest over disparity between the stated and the intended is quite likely to be echoed in many administrative offices and classrooms as state-mandated assessments of teachers acquire varying meanings with each assessment setting and assessor. Assessments have attempted to define measures of competence—and even excellence—for all teachers of all subject matters at all grade levels. It would be naive to assume that a mandated policy will not acquire differential interpretations as it is diffused throughout districts and schools. In chapter 4 Book and Duffy discussed the problematic nature of misusing research findings to assess teachers' communication skills. They considered recent research on students' thought processes that mediate instruction. This chapter will build on their discussion to explore the potential miscommunications to teachers and the general public that may result from current assessment policies.

GENERIC TEACHING BEHAVIORS

In an attempt to control the quality of teaching and, in several states, to reward those teachers who exhibit excellence, the assessors have attempted to interpret "good" or "competent" teaching. With the exception of written tests of subject matter, the assessments discussed by

McCaleb in chapter 1 are deliberately generic in nature. They evaluate all teachers with identical instruments, reducing the potential for district or school biases and permitting comparisons among teachers. This comparative view is particularly important in states such as Texas where the assessment is directly tied to a career ladder and merit pay. The clear implication is that a competent life science teacher in rural Splendora, Texas, will behave similarly to a competent bilingual first-grade teacher in El Paso.

Let us pause for a moment and reflect on this situation with specific reference to communication skills. McCaleb summarized the communication measures into 12 categories: correctness, speech mechanics, fluency, feedback, knowledge of subject matter, explaining, enthusiasm and nonverbal communication, questioning, giving of directions, emphasis, interaction with learners, and interaction with parents. Together these categories suggest that teachers who are skilled classroom communicators are knowledgeable, fluent speakers who are also skilled in interpersonal relations. On the surface, one can find little to argue against this picture of a teacher. The goals expressed by the assessments are well intended and the designers undoubtedly have grappled with defining a good communicator. As the documents are interpreted and amplified by those charged with implementing the assessments, it is important to consider the implicit communications that accompany the efforts to identify and reward quality in teaching. Otherwise, the assessors may be identifying and rewarding something quite different.

Generic teaching behaviors may not produce goal-specific learning. In their attempt to develop instruments to be used with all teachers, many designers have consulted with researchers on effective teaching and have paid close attention to process-product research. This research on teaching that studies the relationships between what teachers *do* and the outcomes of their students (summarized in Brophy & Good, 1986 and in Rosenshine & Stevens, 1986) has identified specific verbal behaviors that tend to increase children's scores on standardized reading and math tests. The process-product research *has* provided educators with a set of practices that are especially useful for enabling students to work through well-structured problems that have correct solutions and lend themselves easily to criterion performance measures. These practices are also useful for helping students develop skills that can be divided into related subskills. They are not applicable, however, for developing the ability to solve ill-structured problems, which have no single answer, or for developing creative thinking or creative expression (Rosenshine & Stevens, 1986). Book and Duffy's critique of the process-product base for assessing communication in chapter 4 indicates that teachers often emphasize task completion instead of developing specific mental strategies. Thus, explicit links between mental activity and task outcome are nonexistent. Teachers can only hope that students will infer those links as a result of task completion.

POSSIBLE MISCOMMUNICATIONS
IMPLIED BY ASSESSMENTS

While the intent to formulate assessments grounded in research on teaching is commendable, there exists the potentially dangerous miscommunication that research has identified behaviors that teachers can follow to guarantee successful teaching. This message, found in the phrase "research says," is communicated overtly and covertly in presentations at professional conferences, training sessions that certify observers and administrators to make the assessments, and briefing sessions for teachers. The phrase is unaccompanied by qualifications identified by the researchers or critiques of the research offered by reviewers.

The process-product research, and hence the assessment instrument, is generically focused as opposed to subject matter focused. Context specific situations and the educational purposes that the instruction may be designed to serve are ignored. There *is* a growing research base on teaching and on effective classroom communication, but that research is a guide for practice rather than a mandate. It is difficult to compare teachers who routinely employ teaching methods that are more student centered and less teacher centered such as creative dramatics, field games in physical education, and inquiry-oriented science programs. Such teachers may depend less on presentational communications and more on interactive communication. In these instructional settings the teacher is less concerned with feedback on "correct" performance and more concerned with challenging, probing, and guiding students toward a qualitative goal of excellence rather than a quantitative goal of test performance. In a search for comparability it is possible that assessments may be sacrificing individual variety and experimentation. The second potential for miscommunication here is that administrators or teachers may limit the universe of desirable communication skills to those being assessed, thereby legitimating only those educational purposes that can be readily assessed by current instrumentation.

A third potential miscommunication resulting from the use of generic instruments is that subject matter is not a consideration when evaluating teaching. For example, in the category that McCaleb identified as feedback, out-of-field observers are expected to judge whether the teacher has appropriately considered the difficulties learners may encounter and taken appropriate steps to alleviate the problem through feedback. An out-of-field observer evaluating physics instruction quality is roughly analogous to a weekend sports fan serving as the home plate umpire in a major league game. The entire quality of the game depends on accuracy of the calls, but the caller cannot quickly and directly identify the distinc-

69

tions between a ball and a strike. One missing program in the history of research on teaching has been the consideration of subject matter (Shulman, 1985). Its absence is even more noteworthy in assessment designs that propose to compare teachers across subject areas, using observers who have little or no knowledge of the subjects being taught.

A fourth miscommunication is the potential for valuing form above content. The problematic nature of communications that emphasize form and style rather than content is a complaint dating back to Plato and Aristotle. Speaking skills and styles can be taught, but communicating so others can understand the content of the communication is quite a different matter. Leinhardt's (1985) study of elementary mathematics instruction documents the differences between knowledgeable elementary math teachers and those who are less knowledgeable. Less knowledgeable teachers tend to rely more on the textbook and give explanations that confuse rather than clarify. It is difficult to understand how the current assessment systems would differentiate between a text dependent (but technically correct) teacher who shows superior vocal ability and a teacher who has mastered the art of explaining a difficult concept but who cannot do so through "intense or dramatic expression in gestures, movements, vocal inflections, or facial changes" (see McCaleb, chapter 1). It would be a dangerous miscommunication if assessments send the message that excellence in teaching is more an issue of form than of subject matter content.

Finally, another potential for miscommunication is that assessments imply teachers are expected to talk more than listen and only teachers can provide feedback or reteach. The observation instruments used in process-product research focused more on teacher behaviors and less on student behaviors, attributing the cause of desirable student outcomes to teacher actions. Critics have argued that all classroom proceedings are mediated by the individual student (Doyle, 1978). Research on students' cognition during instruction (Wittrock, 1986) suggests that there are many different interpretations of instruction. For example, students may be aware when they are not attending to instruction, but they may be unaware that they do not understand a concept or skill. Research on learning and memory (Weinstein & Mayer, 1986) suggests that students must play an active role in instruction and teachers must devise ways to monitor students' progress more closely than can be done through a worksheet exercise. Finding the source of students' errors, informing the students of errors, and providing students with training in metacognitive strategies may be important to helping students in task specific situations not typically measured by standardized tests.

These lines of research suggest that monitoring is a highly complex process that involves more time than a quick check for understanding allows. Helping students shed prior misconceptions in order to understand the correct explanation may take considerable time for diagnosis and reteaching. The process of diagnosis and prescriptive reteaching is closely aligned with subject matter knowledge. Teachers must know the potential for misconceptions and create learning environments that allow those misconceptions to be identified. Teachers are responsible for designing instruction that will enable students to replace the old, incorrect concept with the new, correct concept. Identification, diagnosis, and reteaching require considerable knowledge, pedagogical sophistication, and skill. Expert teachers are flexible enough to alter plans midstream when the occasion demands (Berliner, 1986). This flexibility may not be encouraged to develop through assessments that stress only one form of classroom communication.

The implication is that teachers will need to establish a classroom ethos that does not penalize students for showing the teacher they made a mistake. Students must have learning experiences that will enable them to recognize and correct their errors, either individually or with help from others. Those who understand will have positive educational experiences, but those who do not understand also need to have positive experiences that enable learning to occur.

METAPHORS AND THE ASSESSMENT OF TEACHING

The view of teaching implied by current assessments casts the teacher in the role of a highly skilled actor or actress. Consider McCaleb's 12 categories again. Five—correctness, mechanics, fluency, enthusiasm and nonverbal communication, and emphasis—are directly concerned with vocal and visual performing skills and techniques. The categories that are more interactive—feedback, questioning, giving of direction, interactions with students, and interactions with parents—still focus on the teacher's verbal abilities rather than the teacher's responsibility to develop students' communicative skills. As mentioned earlier, the picture emerges of a knowledgeable, fluent speaker who is also skilled in inter-personal relations. Indeed, several educational researchers have suggested that we train teachers in much the same way that we train actors (Gage, 1978; Travers, 1981). Microteaching and peer teaching could be compared to acting class. But perhaps we are using the wrong metaphor.

The vision of the teacher as actor limits our vision to familiar, albeit idealistic, scenarios of successful teaching in which teachers command center stage and hold the audience's rapt attention while delivering a virtuoso performance. The vocal qualities are evident; the flawless speech is appropriate for the role and captivates and moves the audience. The improvised sections are focused and the meaning is clearly shared among the players. The gestures and facial expressions convey a feeling of excite-ment, which cues audience members who occasionally join in the improvisation as well as those who only observe. Perhaps we are thinking of students as patrons who attend classrooms much as audiences attend the theatre.

But what if we shift the theatrical metaphor and consider the students as actors and the teacher as director? What communication skills could be assessed using this metaphor? And are they congruent with the skills currently being assessed?

An actor is primarily concerned with self; a director is concerned with the total production. That is consistent with the role of the teacher, who must be concerned with the classroom as a whole, including the relationships and the proceedings within the classroom as well as those relationships and proceedings between the class and the school and the class and the community. The actor has limited freedom to interpret the script (and no freedom under some directors). The director, according to Sir Laurence Olivier, "know[s] the play so well that he grasps every important moment of every scene. He knows—and he alone—when the action should rise and where it should fall. He knows where to place the accents" (Cole & Chinoy, 1983, p. 412). The director must also guide the actors as individuals. According to Franco Zeffirelli, "You can't force an actor. He doesn't play with his technique, he plays with his own human qualities. My job is to offer many different solutions to him, and then to choose the right one. It may be comic or tragic, but it must be the right one *for him*. It must become part of his own blood and flesh" (Cole & Chinoy, 1963, p. 438).

Using the director as a metaphor, then, would give increased importance to the relationships between what a teacher plans, knowledge and skill that shape those plans, *students'* responses as those plans are implemented, and a teacher's responses to the students. The classroom observer is forced to probe beneath the surface behaviors recorded on an observation schedule for the intentions of a lesson, consider the teacher's perceptions of how that lesson was implemented, and record how each student worked through the lesson, modifying plans as needed.

FLEXIBLE ASSESSMENT PROCEDURES

It is unnecessary to completely abandon the communication skills currently used. Sets or ranges of alternative behaviors need to be identified, however. The changes should address the miscommunications identified earlier:

1. Research has identified behaviors that teachers can follow to guarantee successful teaching.
2. The universe of desirable communication skills are limited to those being assessed, emphasizing presentational behaviors.
3. Subject matter is not a consideration when evaluating teaching.

4. Excellence in teaching is more an issue of form than of subject matter content.
5. Desirable student outcomes are attributed to teacher actions with little recognition of student mediation.
6. Monitoring is accomplished through a quick check for understanding.
7. Teachers are expected to talk more than listen and only teachers provide feedback or reteach.

The flexible assessment procedures should be consistent with a teacher's purposes and goals and reward teachers for making corrections to the lesson "in flight" if the occasion warranted. A system that allowed time to talk with teachers before the lesson might give an observer richer evidence on interpersonal skills and clue the observer to watch for certain events. Time to talk after the lesson, perhaps to review a videotape of the lesson, would enable a teacher to explain the reasons for decisions that deviated from the original plan. Such deviation is consistent with recent research on expert teaching (Berliner, 1986) that suggests expert teachers function as able executives who can flex to the demands of the immediate classroom situation.

Working with others and helping them to achieve individual goals as well as group goals are more difficult tasks than working alone. The product is more uncertain and the process is unstable and open to continuous negotiation between the concerned parties. There is some evidence from the fledgling research on learning to teach (Doyle, 1985; Grossman, Reynolds, Ringstaff, & Sykes, 1985; Clift & Morgan, 1986) that teacher education coursework and early classroom experiences shift one's focus from self as learner to self as one who directs the learning of others. An assessment system that takes advantage of this focus and provides diagnostic feedback as well as a yearly evaluation would seem to work with teachers rather than against them. And that is the final potential miscommunication that may result from the current assessment systems. Teachers may receive the message that they are not allowed to make mistakes and to learn from them, administrators at all levels are enemies, or professional control is centered in the state capital rather than the classrooms.

Shulman (1983) has argued that, "Educational policies must be designed as a shell within which the kernel of professional judgment and decision making can function comfortably. The policymaker can no longer think of any given mandate as a directive which bears continuing correspondence to teacher action at all times" (p. 501). Assessment policies that communicate respect for the classroom teacher's knowledge combined with implementation plans that include professional development for the directors of student learning will avoid most possibilities for damaging professional miscommunication outlined in this chapter.

References

Berliner, D. C. (1986). In pursuit of the expert pedagogue. *Educational Researcher, 15*(7), 5–13.

Brophy, J. E., & Good, T. L. (1986). Teacher behavior and student achievement. In M. C. Wittrock (Ed.), *Handbook of research on teaching,* (3rd ed.) (pp. 328–375). New York: MacMillan.

Cole, T., & Chinoy, H. C. (1963). *Directors on directing.* Indianapolis, IN: Bobbs Merrill.

Clift, R. T., & Morgan, P. (1986, April). *Future English teacher or English major? Exploring qualitative differences in subject matter knowledge.* Paper presented at the annual meeting of the American Educational Research Association, San Francisco, CA.

Doyle, W. (1978). Paradigms for research on teacher effectiveness. In L. S. Shulman (Ed.), *Review of research in education* (Vol. 5), (pp. 163–198). Itasca, IL: F. E. Peacock.

Doyle, W. (1985). Learning to teach: An emergent direction in research on pre-service teaching. *Journal of Teacher Education 36,*(1), 31–32.

Gage, N. L. (1978). *The scientific basis of the art of teaching.* New York: Teacher's College Press.

Grossman, P., Reynolds, A., Ringstaff, C., & Sykes, G. (1985, April). *English major to English teacher.* Paper presented at the annual meeting of the American Educational Research Association, Chicago, IL.

Leinhardt, G. (1985, April). *The development of an expert explanation: An analysis of a sequence of subtraction lessons.* Paper presented at the annual meeting of the American Educational Research Association, Chicago, IL.

Rosenshine, B., & Stevens, R. (1986). Teaching functions. In M. C. Wittrock (Ed.), *Handbook of research on teaching,* (3rd ed.) (pp. 376–391). New York: MacMillan.

Shulman, L. (1983). Autonomy and obligation: The remote control of teaching. In L. S. Shulman and G. Sykes (Eds.), *Handbook of teaching and policy* (pp. 484–504). New York: Longman.

Shulman, L. S. (1985). Those who understand: Knowledge growth in teaching. *Educational Researcher, 15*(2), 4–14.

Travers, R. M. (1981). Training the teacher as a performing artist., *Contemporary Education, 31*(1), 14–18.

Weinstein, C. F., & Mayer, R. F. (1986). The teaching of learning strategies. In M. C. Wittrock (Ed.), *Handbook of research on teaching,* (3rd ed.) (pp. 315–327). New York: MacMillan.

Wittrock, M. C. (1986). Students' thought processes. In M. C. Wittrock (Ed.), *Handbook of research on teaching,* (3rd ed.) (pp. 297–314). New York, MacMillan.

CONCLUSION

Implications for Improving Communication

While the primary task of this monograph has been to describe and evaluate the conceptualizations of communication found in assessment practices, implications for the *development* of effective communication can also be found. Several recurring conclusions throughout the monograph are summarized below.

1. The assessments of teachers' communication have provided a valuable service in identifying significant dimensions of communication.

The 12 categories described in chapter 1 offer assistance to persons concerned with content validity by defining in precise terms a substantial part of instructional communication's "content universe." Although these categories, even collectively, do not constitute a sufficient conceptualization of communication, they do isolate important dimensions. As is expected of a complex concept in a complex environment, each dimension has the potential of being taken from context and misused. Still, each category appears to have merit in defining a needed component for the repertoire of an effective communicator in an instructional setting. Therefore, the 12 categories should be useful for preservice and/or inservice planners. Other useful resources include Brown's list of books that have been prepared for the improvement of teachers' communications (see p. 43) and the Speech Communication Association's (SCA) annotated bibliographies on sources for improving instructional communication. The SCA also has developed standards for test development (see Appendix).

Most of the authors note that the communication behaviors from these 12 categories are often associated with a linear model of communication; i.e., the emphasis is upon the teacher sending information to the learners. While this emphasis is insufficient for all communication events, it demonstrates some of the most essential behaviors needed by an effective teacher. For example, teachers must be able to present clear explanations. The basic components of effective explanations have been rather well defined (e.g., Cruickshank, 1986; Gage, Belgard, Dell, Hiller, Rosenshine, & Unruh, 1968; McCaleb & Rosenthal, 1984). Researchers have begun to refine the design of training programs for developing teacher clarity (e.g., Book & McCaleb, 1987; Glueckner, 1983; Moore, 1987). Similarly, the concept of monitoring has been refined to a point where explicit training can be presented (see chapter 1).

2. Effectiveness as a communicator demands attention to contextual variables. Perhaps the best illustration of this comes from the research on the effective use of praise. Brophy (1981) illustrates the way that effective communicators make adjustments for learning ability, grade

level, and other student characteristics. Several authors in this monograph also showed that effective instruction in different content fields may require different communication skills.

3. While communication behaviors associated with a linear model of communication (e.g., explaining and mechanics) should be developed, the transactional view of communication must be incorporated into a comprehensive understanding of effective communication. A transactional perspective assumes that communication involves something happening in the classroom that shows a sharing of meaning among teacher and learners rather than just a transfer of information. Transactional communication promotes instructional events that go beyond what is specifically planned by the teacher. Learners are stimulated to propose ideas and insights that were not expected by the teacher, and the teacher gains understandings through the communication process. The transactional perspective poses problems for assessment, but qualitative methodology, including interviews with participants, allows glimpses of it. The particular implication for persons trying to develop effective communication is to see beyond the restrictions of the more easily measured communication behaviors and to enable teachers to understand and to apply a transactional perspective.

4. Authors in this monograph seem particularly excited by the potential relationship between communication and the concept of pedagogical content knowledge. As described in chapter 1, pedagogical content knowledge involves a structure for specific content provided by a teacher in order to effectively present the content to a specific group of learners. This structure differs from the way an expert in the discipline organizes content knowledge. Each chapter contributed to this concept. In chapter 2, the skill area of analyzing the situation promotes the restructuring of content as the teacher incorporates information about learners and curriculum. In order to make the connections with the learners and to restructure content, the teacher uses role taking and adaptive communication as described in chapter 3. Part of the adaptive communication is the modeling of thought, discussed by Book and Duffy in chapter 4. Chapter 5 notes that feedback should reflect fine-tuning associated with content expertise.

5. Other points made in individual chapters merit the attention of those trying to improve the communication of teachers. For example, in chapter 2, Feezel emphasizes the willingness or motivation to communicate, a dimension relatively ignored in assessment and assistance. Teacher education programs might assist teachers in gaining an understanding of their attitudes toward communication and the effects of those attitudes on learners (McCroskey, 1977). For example, an extroverted high school teacher might increase empathy with the student who is afraid to talk, even to peers. Feezel also shows the relevance of the functional approach.

A SCA subcommittee report (Cooper, 1986) elaborates this approach, identifying competencies in the five functional areas.

In chapter 3, Brown develops the role of language in teaching. As teachers increase awareness of specialized terminology used in their content fields and in pedagogical language, they can construct more considerate definitions and explicit instruction. Closely related is the notion of conceptual consistency developed by Book and Duffy in chapter 4. Learning can be enhanced when teachers distinguish significant points from illustrative material and then cue these differences for learners periodically. Again, preservice and inservice efforts can contribute by identifying the significant points, polishing strategies for emphasizing these points, and promoting teachers' awareness of how and when they emphasize the significant material.

Finally, chapter 5 provides a means of synthesis with an instructive metaphor. The teacher is often, even if implicitly, conceptualized as a performer, an actor. Clift shifts the theatrical metaphor to the director. This metaphor advances the varied communication roles needed by the teacher: the teacher knows the content more broadly than from one role; the teacher makes important design decisions; and, perhaps most critically, the teacher takes risks in creating a successful production.

77

References

Book, C. L., & McCaleb, J. L. (1987). *Relationships of clarity and instructional explicitness, student awareness, and classroom management.* Unpublished manuscript, Michigan State University.

Brophy, J. (1981). Teacher praise: A functional analysis. *Review of Educational Research. 51*, 5–32.

Cooper, P. J. (1986). *Communication Competencies for Teachers: A CAT Subcommittee Report.* Chicago, IL: Speech Communications Association. (ERIC Document Reproduction Service No. SP 028 649)

Cruickshank, D. R., & Kennedy, J. J. (1986). Teacher clarity. *Teaching and Teacher Education, 2,* 43–67.

Gage, N. L., Belgard, M., Dell, D., Hiller, J. E., Rosenshine, B., & Unruh, W. R. (1968). *Explorations of the teacher's effectiveness in explaining* (Tech. Rep. No. 2). Stanford: Stanford University, School of Education.

Glueckner, G. (1983). *An investigation into the effectiveness of a preservice teacher clarity training unit in two different experimental settings.* Unpublished doctoral dissertation, The Ohio State University.

McCaleb, J. L., & Rosenthal, B. G. (1984). Relationships in teacher clarity between students' perceptions and observers' ratings. *Journal of Classroom Interaction, 19* (1), 15–21.

McCroskey, J. C. (1977). *Quiet children and the classroom teacher.* Annandale, VA: Speech Communication Association.

Moore, N. J. (1987). *Effects of a training program in clarity for secondary preservice teachers.* Unpublished doctoral dissertation, University of Maryland.

APPENDIX

SCA CRITERIA FOR EVALUATING INSTRUMENTS AND PROCEDURES FOR ASSESSING SPEAKING AND LISTENING

The following criteria may be applied to published and unpublished instruments and procedures for assessing speaking and listening skills of children and adults. These guidelines are presented here together with information describing how users of speaking and listening assessment instruments can use the procedures in a manner consistent with accepted testing practices. Originally published in 1980, the criteria (1986) have been revised to conform to the Educational Testing Service's published guidelines on appropriate test use. The criteria are organized in a manner consistent with ETS standards.

A. Purposes of Testing. As the purposes of educational testing vary widely, the following criteria describe the Speech Communication Association's position on the purposes of assessing speaking and listening skills. It is critically important to the testing procedure that the purpose of the testing be well defined before a test is developed or adopted. Lack of a match between purpose and instrument may lead to invalid test results.

1. Stimulus materials should require the individual being tested to *demonstrate* skill as a speaker or listener.

2. Assessment instruments and procedures should clearly distinguish speaking and listening performance from reading and writing ability; i.e., inferences of speaking and listening competence should not be made from tests of reading and writing, and directions and responses for speaking and/or listening tests should not be mediated through reading and writing modes.

3. Assessment should confirm the degree to which a skill is present or absent, and not diagnose reasons why individuals demonstrate or fail to demonstrate those skills.

4. Assessment should emphasize the application of speaking and listening skills to familiar situations, i.e., stimulus materials should refer to situations recognizable to the individual being tested and should facilitate demonstration of skills rather than demonstration of mastery of a specified content.

5. Any assessment of oral skills should reflect more than one communication setting (e.g., interpersonal, small group, public, and mass communication settings) rather than be a generalization about skills when only one setting is used.

B. Qualification of Test Users. Necessary qualifications of test users vary with the test or assessment procedure being used. Many assessment procedures can be effectively administered by the classroom teacher. Other procedures require a varying degree of training on the part of the test administrator, and many testing procedures require training in speech communication. What is most important is that every test administrator in a given testing program receive enough training and practice with the assessment procedure to ensure adequate rater reliability. When a testing procedure is being considered for use, careful attention should be paid to the requirements regarding the administration of the test.

C. Test Selection. In addition to the criteria described in the other sections of this document, the following criteria are suggested by SCA to aid in selecting an appropriate test.

   1. Assessment instruments should be free of sexual, cultural, racial, and ethnic content and/or stereotyping.
   2. Assessment should permit a range of *acceptable* responses, where such a range is appropriate.
   3. Assessment should demonstrate that outcomes are more than just chance evidence; i.e., assessment should be reliable.
   4. Assessment should provide results that are consistent with other evidence that might be available.
   5. Assessment should have content validity.
   6. Assessment should be suitable for the developmental level of the individual being tested.

D. Test Administration. The following criteria speak to the guidelines suggested by SCA regarding test administration. Together with the information on the qualifications of test users, these criteria provide assistance on test use and administration.

   1. Assessment procedures should be standardized and detailed enough so that individual responses will not be affected by the administrator's skills in administering the procedures.
   2. Assessment procedures should approximate the recognized stress level of oral communication; the procedures and setting should not increase or eliminate it.
   3. Assessment procedures should be practical in terms of cost and time.
   4. Assessment should involve simple equipment.

E. Scoring Tests. Each testing procedure should use a standardized score sheet to record the ratings. Most assessment procedures include scoring instructions. If the test scores are to be used for purposes other than feedback to the individual student, then summary sheets should be constructed that ensure testee anonymity.

F. Interpreting Test Scores. Interpretation of test scores may be the province of the individual teacher or other administrator. If there are not national norms for the speaking/listening assessment procedure, cut-off scores for use in placement, development of educational objectives, remediation, etc. should be set and agreed upon by the appropriate teachers/administrators. Scores should also reflect the nature of the context for conditions used in the test.

G. Communicating Test Results. Under normal circumstances, individual test results should be considered confidential information. Individual scores should be communicated to the students and/or parents in a confidential manner. Use of test scores for the development of test norms for educational objectives or for trend analysis should be accomplished while maintaining individual test score confidentiality. Test results should only be reported in a way that explains the nature of the levels being reported.

H. Handling of Data. Data should be handled in accordance with F and G above. Procedures for handling data should be developed to fit local needs. Assessment should occur immediately prior to the use of the ratings or scores so that data are current. Data may be retained in student records but should be considered as potentially obsolete after one year.

I. Monitoring Compliance with Guidelines. Each school, district, or institution using a testing procedure in speaking and listening should appoint an individual whose duties include periodic checks to see that raters are following the testing procedures accurately, that scores are being dealt with appropriately, and that complaints or disputes are handled expediently.

Criteria developed (1980) by Philip M. Backlund, Kenneth L. Brown, Joanne Gurry, and Fred E. Jandt acting as a subgroup of the Speech Communication Association's Committee on Assessment and Testing. Approved and endorsed by the Educational Policies Board and the Administrative Committee of the Speech Communication Association. Revised, December 1986, under the direction of the SCA's Committee on Assessment and Testing's standards subcommittee, Philip M. Backlund, Chair; Members Rebecca Rubin and Don Boileau.

About the Authors

Cassandra L. Book is assistant dean of the College of Education at Michigan State University and professor of teacher education. She is active in both communication and education professional associations and has published extensively in the areas of communication education, instructional communication, and teacher education. As a senior researcher in the Institute for Research on Teaching, she collaborated on a series of studies on explicit instruction of low group readers.

Kenneth L. Brown is a professor of communication and assistant dean in the College of Arts and Sciences at the University of Massachusetts, Amherst. He has directed teacher education programs in communication for 26 years. A past chairperson of the Speech Communication Association's Educational Policies Board and former editor of *Communication Education,* he has coauthored two books on children's communication development and authored numerous articles on teaching and assessing oral communication and classroom communication.

Renee T. Clift, assistant professor in the Department of Curriculum & Instruction at the University of Houston, formerly taught high school English, speech, and drama. Her current research focuses on the process of learning to teach English language arts, the development of a knowledge base for teaching, and the teacher's role in acquiring strategic study skills. She is involved in developing the Reflective Inquiry Teacher Education Program at the University of Houston.

Gerald G. Duffy, professor of education in the College of Education at Michigan State University, taught in elementary and junior high schools. He conducts research on classroom instruction and teacher thinking and publishes regularly in numerous professional journals. His major interest is instructional improvement and helping teachers assume control of their instruction.

Jerry D. Feezel, professor of speech communication at Kent State University, heads the undergraduate and graduate programs in speech education and coordinates two basic speech communication courses. He is a former high school speech and English teacher and past president of the Ohio Speech Communication Association. He has written two books, book chapters, and articles on teacher education, language, and interpersonal communication.

82

Joseph L. McCaleb is an associate professor at the University of Maryland with a joint appointment in the Department of Curriculum & Instruction and the Department of Communication Arts & Theater. He has taught speech, theater, and English in junior high and high school. His research on instructional communication has emphasized the investigation of teacher clarity and has been published in several journals. He has chaired a Speech Communication Association committee on the assessment of teachers' communications and is currently on the faculty of an experimental fifth-year teacher education program.